THE
LAST GREAT RIDE

THE
LAST GREAT RIDE

Brandon Tartikoff
and Charles Leerhsen

Turtle Bay Books

A Division of Random House

New York

1992

ISBN: 0-394-58709-X
LC: 91-58087

Manufactured in the United States of America
24689753
First Edition

To the three women in my life—
Lilly, Calla, and my mother, Enid.
Your love of life, your love of me,
and your incredible courage
inspire me every day.

And to my father, Jordan,
for teaching me how to be strong by example.

CONTENTS

BACKSTORY

....

Imagine, if you will, a seven-year-old boy sitting nose-to-screen in front of a seven-inch DuMont television set, mesmerized by everything he sees. To him, this television set is pure magic. He begins to fantasize that if he tried hard he could shrink to a tiny size and crawl inside the set. Then he could live and breathe television from the inside, all day.

That boy got his wish.

When I was a kid and my lifelong fascination with television was budding, my favorite show, the one I most looked forward to seeing every Sunday night, was *The Ed Sullivan Show*. At our household (as well as millions of others), *The Ed Sullivan*

Show was the punctuation point of the week. It signaled that the weekend (fun) was about to go dark, and Monday (schoolwork) was about to begin. It also meant that no matter where my family had scattered during the weekend, we would all reassemble in front of that DuMont set to see Ed dazzle us with everything from jugglers to opera singers to comics to rock 'n' roll stars.

Most kids grow up wanting to have glamorous and exciting jobs—professional athlete, president, jet pilot, doctor. All I ever wanted to be was Ed Sullivan. (Oh sure, I secretly wished I could be the third baseman for the Dodgers, yet how realistic was that when I was hitting .267 in Little League?) But Ed Sullivan—his job didn't seem out of reach. Here was a man who couldn't sing, couldn't dance, and, try as he might, couldn't tell a joke. Still, he had his own television show where he could present the most talented people in the world to everybody in America.

At age ten I rigged up a tape recorder to create my own backyard PA system, and began broadcasting live every night: the Delinquent Deejay of Delaware Avenue in Freeport, Long Island. The neighbors complained. I persisted. And my father deep-sixed the tape recorder to the bowels of our basement.

By the time I was graduating from college into the workplace in 1970, Ed Sullivan was about to end his twenty-three-year run on CBS.

Technically then, there was no more *Ed Sullivan Show,* so how could I be Ed? My ambition had to be rechanneled.

I was assigned a book to review for a free-lance gig I had with *The New Haven Register.* The book was called *The Business Behind the Box,* written by *Variety* guru Les Brown. Brown chronicled the adventures and many accomplishments of Fred Silverman, the head of programming at CBS. Fred was a young guy then, in his early thirties, brimming with talent and an insatiable curiosity about television shows, all kinds of television shows. Every day he worked with the most talented performers in the world and presented them to America. *He* got to play television. In a way, he was just like Ed Sullivan. "Why not?" I thought to myself. "I can do that." More to the point, I *wanted* to do that.

And so I did. Not right away, mind you, but after spending the first half of the seventies in local television, I got to take my game to a higher level, to play in the majors. And who should be my Branch Rickey? None other than a man who wouldn't know who Branch Rickey was: Fred Silverman.

In 1980, after apprenticing under Fred, first at ABC, and then for three years at NBC, I in effect got my own show: I got to be the head of programming at one of the major networks. The one with the peacock.

The show ran for twelve years, a good stretch regardless of what metaphor you use. It's not to say the show was a hit from the start. Like a lot of programs I would later be associated with, success was slow in coming. But when I left NBC in 1991, we had been number one in the ratings for six consecutive seasons. I got to leave a winner.

When I was fortunate enough to be promoted to the top programming job at NBC in 1980, I was told that at age thirty-one I was the youngest person who had ever held the position. When I left last year at age forty-two, I realized I had held the position longer than anyone else in television history by four years. Those two records will fall certainly sometime in the near future. With so many young, talented people out there, it's just a matter of time. But the record I do want to own into the next millennium is a little harder to quantify. I'd like to be remembered as the person who had the most fun doing the job of playing television.

Why am I so serious about having fun? Well, no matter how hard the task of turning out good programs, or how increasingly severe the financial constraints in doing so, the maxim immemorial of television remains blatantly true: "If you're having a good time making it, they'll have a good time watching it."

Four years ago, in the midst of NBC's historic prime-time winning streak, I was approached to do this book. A lot has changed since then. For one thing, I've changed jobs. It's always hard to know when to get off the stage, especially when the audience is still applauding. Bob Wright, that rare hyphenate, my boss-friend, offered many innovative scenarios to keep me as part of the team. But after twelve years of overnights and forty pilots a year—after fending off the Reverend Donald Wildmon, affiliates, and nervous-nelly advertisers—it was time to move on. As Fred Silverman once told me, "You know it's time to turn the job over when you're starting a new season and the ideas that you're most interested in doing are all the ones that didn't work last season."

I'm now the chairman of Paramount Studios, a position I accepted in the spring of 1991. I still get to play television with the shows we produce: *Cheers, Young Indiana Jones, Brooklyn Bridge, Star Trek: The Next Generation,* and *The Arsenio Hall Show.* But now I get to help project visions on the big screen that can't be fully realized on the tube. Like *The Addams Family* and *Wayne's World.* ("That was a joke!" as Milton Berle would say. "Are you an audience or an oil painting?")

For another thing, television has changed. The technology revolution caused VCRs, cable, and the expansion of independent station channels to redefine the competitive landscape of broadcasting. And the revolution rages on in the nineties. Soon high definition television, interactive programs, and digitalization will totally transform the ways in which we look at and receive television. Whether those innovations will nullify the truth in Bruce Springsteen's song "57 Channels (and Nothin' On)" remains to be seen. And yes, my alma mater NBC has changed. But that was inevitable, and in a way I was forewarned. At the farewell dinner for outgoing NBC chairman Grant Tinker, I congratulated him on having just about the best five-year run anybody could have had in the network game. To which he replied, "Brandon, it was a broadcast. It's like building sand castles. We build them elaborately and beautifully, but eventually they just get washed away."

The title of this book, *The Last Great Ride,* was conjured up back in 1988. It was not meant as an act of hubris on my part, but as an acknowledgment that the medium has changed so irrevocably. Even when the next television dynasty comes about, that network or other entity will never captivate the imagination and consciousness of the country as we were fortunate enough to do in the eighties. No one is going to average an 18 weekly rating and have that kind of hold on the audience. No one is likely to have the wherewithal to do the things we did, because no one is likely to have the money we did during our glorious run.

But *The Last Great Ride* almost became the title, albeit a horrifically ironic one, of a posthumous memoir.

On New Year's Day in 1991 I was driving my daughter, Calla, for a little afternoon bowling when our Jeep was hit by a speeding car while traversing a highway in Lake Tahoe. We both suffered significant injuries, hers far worse than mine. Whereas I arrived at the hospital in Reno cut up and blood-ied, my daughter had not a scratch. What she did have was a head injury that put her in a coma for six weeks.

Ever since that fateful day my wife's and my mission in life is to get Calla back to where she was before the accident. A year and a half later she is well on her way toward that goal. Not because her parents willed it or wanted it, but because she worked for it. She has endured a seven-day-a-week physi-cal therapy ordeal that would test a marine. With never a complaint and always an incredibly positive spirit.

Because of her courage and her steady progress toward a full recovery, I was emotionally able to finish the book that I had nearly completed before the accident.

Before I got into the business, I sometimes found myself gazing up at my set and wondering how certain wretched programs had ever come to pass. Other times I would be awestruck by a consistently great series or spectacular minise-ries. Having now been there, I thought there was a value in telling you how both occurrences are not only possible, but probable. I wanted to let you see what it's like to be in the programmer's hot seat.

The first time I ever saw a magic act was on (you guessed it) *The Ed Sullivan Show*. I never could figure out how those magicians did what they did. I was told that the great ones never tell their secrets or reveal their tricks.

When it comes to the magic that comes through the television set, I never felt the secrets or the tricks were so extraordinary that they couldn't be shared. They are, in fact, just the roadside attractions along *The Last Great Ride*.

THE
LAST GREAT RIDE

ONE

....

The Best Worst Job
in the World

Ⅰt is 11:45 one night in January of 1984. My daughter, Calla, then in the midst of her terrible twos, wakes up my wife, Lilly, and me. She can't sleep. The three of us sit there in our bedroom wide-eyed and at loose ends. I turn on *The Tonight Show*, and see that Joan Rivers is the host. It reminds me that I'm scheduled to have lunch in a few days with Johnny Carson. Then Joan snaps me back to reality by saying, "Let's bring him out, folks: Bill Cosby."

As Cosby goes into his monologue, my initial thought is: This man is a stand-up comedian like Einstein was a physics whiz. Although he is hardly old, Cosby strikes me—tonight more than ever before—as being from the tradition of Jackie Gleason, Red Skelton, Jack Benny, and Bob Hope: a link to an era when giants walked the earth. Those guys could do it all, I'm thinking—work nightclubs, act in movies, make records, and write books—but, ah, they're a dying breed. Then, just as I finish composing this term paper for the George Jessel School of Celebrity Eulogizing, I notice that Cosby has completely reworked his act. He's not talking about Fat Albert or sleeping in the same bed with six of his brothers anymore, he's talking about being an adult, the father of adolescent children, the husband of a woman he met twenty years ago but is still getting to know. His stories are rooted in the real world—one is about his neighbor's daughter getting pregnant, having the baby, and then going off to college and leaving her parents with the kid. He manages to be contemporary without being caustic. Cosby himself, in fact, seems to have mellowed along with his material: I don't see the anger, just behind his eyes, that made me a little uncomfortable when I watched him on *The Tonight Show* just a few years ago.

Suddenly various wheels are spinning in my head. I'm thinking of the *Newsweek* cover story I just saw on the New Baby Boom. It's been hot news that Yuppies are pouring out of their fern bars to nest and propagate—that the generation of free love is suddenly thinking in terms of expensive schools, home remodeling, getting old, parenting, commitments, and other subjects that Cosby is now nailing to the wall in his act.

Meanwhile, in another part of my brain, I am zapping the background file on Bill Cosby. I can recall, of course, his mid-sixties hit, *I Spy*; *The Bill Cosby Show*, in which he played a phys-ed teacher; plus two equally forgettable variety hours.

"It's amazing how this guy hasn't had another hit show, considering he has one of the most known and loved faces on TV. His commercial work alone has kept his face in front of television audiences longer than anyone I can think of," I say to Lilly—who doesn't respond, having fallen back asleep, along with Calla. I, meanwhile, am more awake now than I've been all day. My heart is pounding, my mind is going into overdrive.

Remember how you used to feel back in school the night before you got your report card—that queasiness in the pit of your stomach, that wave of nausea? Well, that's how I went to bed many nights for twelve years. That's not to say I couldn't sleep at all, but even in sleep there was no escape. You see, I *dreamed* television. Shows, concepts, pitch meetings, power breakfasts. Freud would not have been taxed trying to figure out what was going on here.

Television was my *life*, but breathing, eating, and sleeping television can, in many ways, be a living hell. After all, I had been the kid who dreamed of climbing inside the tiny set in my parent's room and getting to play TV. So if the poet was right and hell *is* the place where you get everything you ever wanted, I guess I got my just deserts.

For twelve years, I had the best worst job in the world.

It was the best job because it came with almost God-like power. When you're head of a network's entertainment division, you can get the germ of an idea that might lead to *The Cosby Show*, help make it real, and then see it pumped into 50 million homes. Or put a show like *Miami Vice* on the air, then watch the men of America stop shaving and wearing socks.

Here was the authority to green-light *An Early Frost,* the first television movie about AIDS, and push for *Adam,* which made a nation conscious of the perils of missing children; the ability to look a cop-show producer in the eye, tap a script with my index finger, and say, "I want you to kill off the crack dealer in the second act." And yes, you can even play God and kill off a lead character in a series. This is exactly what happened, for example, in *Valerie.* And the show lived on for another three years. Publicly, all that changed was the title of the show. It became *The Hogan Family.* Privately, the staff called it "Throw Momma from the Series."

But my job was also the worst job in the world because television is a monster that keeps screaming "Feed me!" The men and women in charge of network programming have to oversee twenty-five prime-time series each year, and thirty made-for-television movies, not to mention miniseries and specials. They have to come up with new ideas to supplant the ones that are suddenly sagging and showing their age. Just the addition of Kirstie Alley gave *Cheers* a facelift, and the show is still going strong five years later. Right now *Designing Women,* in its second year of revamping, is still trying to recapture the kind of chemistry it had when it premiered six years ago. (One sure sign of an aging sitcom: The producers resort to an episode about Dad finding the teenage daughter's birth-control pills.) These network executives have to make sure their soap operas aren't burning out their popular characters and that the kid shows on Saturday morning haven't become the video equivalent of the Hula Hoop.

Because television is a game, a game in which you can keep score in various ways: Nielsen ratings, corporate profits, an inner sense of having done good work. And as much as those of us in television—producers, directors, writers, etc.—feel like tearing our hair out when one of our favorite shows gets killed in the ratings, threatening the corporate bottom line, winning is the only way you get to keep playing. And the secret of winning is that you have to become completely obsessed. Because ultimately—no matter how good a team you've assembled, and I for one had a great team—you're the one responsible for it all.

Yet even the huge workload was part of the fun. I *wanted* to do it all, even if I couldn't, really—and I wasn't happy until NBC had all its shows arrayed before the public on their proper days and in their best time slots. Scheduling is vital to a network's success. And scheduling was one of the things I was thinking about that fateful night I caught Bill Cosby on *The Tonight Show.* Having a strong show like *Cosby* at eight o'clock could be the start of a perfect TV night—something that depends on grabbing the audience early and providing the maximum "viewer flow" from one time slot to the next. Marty Starger, who was head of programming at ABC when I began working there, used to say that you should program a night so that a certain type of viewer can start out with you at the beginning of the evening and stay with you until the end. In other words, you don't want to open at eight o'clock with a younger-female-oriented sitcom like *Full House,* then schedule an older-male-oriented show like *America's Most Wanted* at nine o'clock, followed by a nighttime serial like *Knots Landing* or *Sisters* at ten o'clock. It's just common sense, of course, to have one show gathering an audience for what comes next. Still, scheduling isn't as simple as it sounds.

Nowhere in these pages will you find the Seven Golden Rules of Great Television, and for good reason. There are no rules. Nor are there any consistent management tactics, because the moment you get consistent in this business, the party's over; you've blown the job. Most TV shows are contracted out to creative independent producers, and if you're in charge of programming you have to radically alter the amount of "managing" each one of those producers gets.

Over time, a good programmer or television executive learns to use power creatively. Who said, "Power is the ability to give others power"? Whoever did, I believe it. On TV series such as *Hill Street Blues, Cheers,* and *Seinfeld,* you find uniquely talented visionaries and use your power to keep those people motivated and happy, and to keep their shows protected in as good a time slot as you can find. With shows like *Knight Rider, Facts of Life,* and other equally popular audience pleasers, you often play a different role. You and your team of executives are, in effect, a triage unit that regularly performs life support on the programs, encouraging the producers to create topical story lines based on the headlines of the day, stunt-cast promotable personalities (such as pop icons), or create *TV Guide* log lines that will sound enticing.

In short, you have to know where to pounce, as well as when and how hard.

This is not an easy thing to pull off. Every network head had more whopping failures than successes, and I certainly had my share of both—as you shall see. But like they say in baseball: It's a long season. You hang in there, then hang in there some more, and sometimes things change. Ultimately, I was part of a unique era in TV history, a strange and wonderful period when NBC advanced the boundaries of TV as we knew them and also kicked some serious Nielsen-ratings butt.

In the eighties, we went from being dead last with an inverted bullet to becoming the most successful—and profitable—network in history. For one glorious stretch that lasted so long that some people began to consider it unseemly—sixty-eight weeks—we ranked first in the prime-time ratings, a record that may forever stand. I certainly can't take sole credit for NBC's great turnaround. I was fortunate enough to be the captain of a great team of executives, a television dynasty comparable to the one the Mings had in China or the Yankees had in 1927. But I was there, in the boardrooms, and on the soundstages, too. And what I saw there was sometimes funnier, more dramatic and more interesting, than what went out over the airwaves.

Let me conjure up a moment from the bad old days, the time before the big turnaround began.

My boss at the time, Fred Silverman, was a legendary TV figure who was constantly in the midst of revamping our programs, from *Hello, Larry* and *B.J. and the Bear,* for example, to *Real People* and *Hill Street Blues.*

One day I walked into Fred's office and said, "You know, it's occurred to me that TV is like a department store. If you're K mart and you want to become Saks Fifth Avenue, you can't do it overnight. If you were known for vacuum cleaners and Fruit of the Loom and now you want to sell cashmere sweaters and Gucci shoes, then there's going to be a period where the customers have to adjust to what you're doing. I think at the moment this network is K mart trying to become Saks."

Fred leaned back in his office chair and waited for me to finish. Then he looked at me and said, "That's a very nice theory, Brandon, but actually what we need here are some goddamn *hits.*"

And of course he was right about that. TV, at bottom, is like almost any other endeavor. You get ahead by getting ahead. It's that first goddamn hit that's the hardest. Which brings me back, of course, to Bill Cosby.

One thing that got me so excited while watching Cosby perform was that I could actually envision a deal happening and a show reaching the airwaves. Jerry Katzman, then the head of television for the William Morris Agency, had been shopping Cosby around, in a laid-back sort of way, for about two years. It would take a substantial commitment to get Bill to come off the road and quit his lucrative schedule of stage performances, Katzman said, but there were some ideas he might be willing to try. The concepts Katzman suggested— one had Cosby as a rich, eccentric detective—were, to put it mildly, nothing to come off the road about. But at least they indicated that the star was primed to brave the prime-time waters again.

The next morning I call Katzman to tell him that I am interested in a Cosby show—"but only," I caution, "if it's rooted in Bill Cosby's real life." I know, instantly, that we have the makings of a deal because Katzman segues gracefully into that eternal question: Who will produce? This choice is especially crucial because while film is a director's medium, the producer is most important in television. A good idea in bad hands inevitably fails. (The converse is also true.) In a case like *Cosby,* the basic idea is so simple that execution will be key. Katzman's fortuitous suggestion for the production auspice is the team of Marcy Carsey and Tom Werner, former network executives at ABC who are coincidentally, clients of his and who, also coincidentally, have developed a treatment for a situation comedy starring Bill Cosby. Marcy, Tom, and I have had a good relationship since we all worked together in the late seventies at ABC. So I agree to proceed, and a few days later I learn, through Katzman, that Cosby is saying, "Let's take things to the next level," too. That chugga-chugga you hear is the train pulling out of the station.

The next level, however, is a problem. Carsey and Werner have a deal with ABC that gives that network the right of first refusal on their next project. Suppose ABC doesn't refuse? I'm thinking. Suppose they like the idea we helped form, put it on the air, and then reap all the rewards? I don't know if Carsey and Werner agreed with me; it wasn't my place to discuss their contractual obligations with another network. But somehow, when they went to see Lew Erlicht, my counterpart at ABC, they left his office without a commitment. I was slightly amazed by this, because Lew is a very sharp guy. And he got not one but two chances to have the show.

That came about because of the financial realities of network TV. *Cosby* was not the kind of show you paid for out of petty cash. I had agreed to give Carsey and Werner a commitment for six episodes so they could get going on the scripts, but we still had a huge hurdle in front of us. The licensing fee Carsey-Werner Productions needed was a very expensive (at that time) $400,000 per episode, a number that reflected the star's salary, the salary of the producers, and the fact that Cosby wanted to tape the show in New York, where he lived.

It should be noted that in the corporate culture of broadcasting the influence of the business affairs department is in inverse proportion to the amount of programming success currently being enjoyed at a network. In other words, when a large percentage of your shows are hits, the programming people have more of the power; when most of your shows are bombs, business affairs gets to flex their muscles.

Unfortunately for me and my programming colleagues at NBC, the birthing process of the *Cosby* show was coming on the heels of the infamous September Train Wreck of 1983, a disaster in which not one of our nine new fall series lived to make the cold weather. It's practically a decade since that season of our discontent, but I can still recite our version of the Catonsville Nine: *Manimal, Mr. Smith, We Got It Made, Jennifer Slept Here, The Rousters, The Yellow Rose, For Love and Honor, The Bay City Blues,* and *Boone.*

You may not remember these shows, but believe me, *I* remember them. Oh, that I didn't.

In other words, business affairs was not exactly throwing giant sums of money in my direction when I told them about the show. I could do it, they said, but the price they came up with was $30,000 an episode less than what the producers wanted. I had no choice but to tell Carsey and Werner that if they didn't like our price they were free to shop the show around elsewhere. "Our business guys aren't playing poker with you," I said. "This is their final offer."

Sleep did not come easily for the next two weeks. Carsey-

Werner's next move was to bring the show back to ABC. This time Lew Erlicht, who as I say is no fool, liked what he heard. But fortunately for me, ABC was a network with different rules. No one who had failed in his past few television attempts received a commitment for twenty-two, thirteen, or even one episode unless he or she successfully auditioned the show first. With a pilot. Bill Cosby didn't want to audition. So the producers came back to NBC, the only other network that had expressed interest in the show, and worked out a deal with us. I breathed a giant sigh of relief.

About three years later, a soon-to-be-famous story about Erlicht's response to all this surfaced: Erlicht was walking down the street in New York with Bill Haber, an agent from the Creative Artists Agency, when a homeless person approached him. "Hey," the guy said, "can you help me out? I'm in really desperate shape." "Listen," Lew replied as he kept on walking, "don't give me *your* sad story. I'm the guy who passed on *The Cosby Show.*"

You've heard of "high concept." (Any show whose premise I had to explain more than once to the NBC sales department.) *The Cosby Show*, however, was still in its low-concept phase. Carsey and Werner had corralled the tremendous talents of Jay Sandrich (the director) and Ed. Weinberger and Michael Leeson (cowriters) to work with Cosby on creating a 15-minute pilot consisting of selected scenes from the show. But beyond that we still didn't know very much about what *The Cosby Show* would look, sound, or feel like on the screen. That meant it was time for a process known as "development."

But development for *The Cosby Show* did not go smoothly. Just because the show had a simple premise didn't mean that there weren't a lot of decisions to be made. One question that had to be resolved fairly quickly was the profession of Bill Cosby's character. After everyone had considered—and rejected—the idea of Cosby as a working-class guy struggling to meet the mortgage (just wouldn't ring true) or as a Las Vegas entertainer (not lovable enough), Bill himself came up with the idea of playing an obstetrician, a character that would be based on a doctor friend of his. How big the Cosby household would be on the show was another question that we debated. Should Cosby's aging parents live under the same roof with him? And where should that roof be—in Atlanta or New York? Ultimately, thank goodness, the idea of keeping the characters true to Cosby's real life prevailed.

The NBC troika of Tartikoff, Jeff Sagansky (now head of CBS Entertainment), and Warren Littlefield (now head of NBC Entertainment) felt strongly that we should keep things simple. "Let's keep it close to Cosby's life," we kept saying, until everyone capitulated, tearfully. Okay, I'm exaggerating, but only a little. We believed the simplicity theme needed to be constantly stressed. At one point, the pilot pitch had Cosby as a New Yorker transplanted to Atlanta, with his wife and children as well as his own mother and father—three generations under one roof. "Why do you need all those complications?" I said. "If you want grandparents, they can visit. And how many stories are you going to get out of the fact that somebody wants to see ballet or good theater and they're not getting it in Atlanta? What's wrong with a simple idea?"

We felt even stronger about Cosby not playing down in

terms of socioeconomic class. Bill didn't usually take part in the development meetings himself—few stars do; but one day very early in the discussions he had Carsey-Werner convey the message that he'd been thinking his character should be a chauffeur married to a domestic. We thought that was probably the single biggest mistake we could make. "America knows and loves Bill Cosby as a successful black man who's very comfortable with his status and material success," I said to Tom and Marcy. "Cosby wearing old clothes and taking a second job to pay the mortgage just won't ring true."

Of course, once the show made its debut, many people thought we overdid it—that the Huxtables had much too lush a life. For a while it was almost fashionable in some quarters to criticize the show for being unrealistic and overly upbeat. Cliff, Clair, and the kids were said to be a tad too cozy in their Brooklyn brownstone: Their incomes were too substantial, their family life too happy and secure. These critics of *Cosby* felt that we, the people deep down inside the tube, were projecting an ideal that could never be realized, and that could only lead to massive disappointment and regret.

I've heard that argument many times; I understand the logic, but I don't agree with it at all. I think *The Cosby Show* made people feel good. And I believe the show worked because it was more realistic than most other sitcoms. In the Huxtable household, big problems didn't get resolved in the usual twenty-two minutes. In fact, the show usually didn't deal with the Big Problems that cropped up in so many other sitcoms. Instead, it dealt with small problems and the small but memorable moments that can make up American family life.

Cosby himself was adamant about stressing what he called "the universality of experience." The characters may have been black, but no one ever got a cheap laugh by burlesquing his racial identity. Even the show's rhythms played off real life, with scenes dovetailing into each other naturally—sort of slice-of-life storytelling rather than plot-driven, standard sitcom fare. Bill not only broke new ground in the manner in which black families were portrayed on television, but also paved the way for another accomplished monologuist, Jerry Seinfeld, to take a slice of his own life and turn it into one of the best comedies on the air today.

In the end, the show that depended entirely on execution was executed very well indeed. The continuing saga of Dr. Cliff Huxtable, his attorney wife, Clair, and their five children made its debut on NBC on September 20, 1984. The next morning I got up in L.A. at six o'clock, called Nancy Mead, the person in New York who had the thankless task of giving manic-depressive executives the overnight ratings, and braced myself. A smash in those days was anything above a 30 share, and at NBC we'd hire a deejay and tap a keg of beer if a show premiered in double digits. I had high hopes for *Cosby*—maybe a 27.

What Nancy said to me was, "Well, Brandon, in the nine overnight markets that have reported in so far, the show averaged a forty-eight."

"I've gotten fours before, and I've had eights," I said. "But the two *together*?"

The value of a show that grabs the top spot in the ratings and then holds it for eight years, the way *Cosby* did, can't be calculated. The millions NBC made from selling commercial spots on *Cosby* was just the beginning of the bonanza. Any show that followed it benefited tremendously, as did the entire Thursday evening lineup. *Cosby* also gave NBC newfound cachet in the creative community. It encouraged the best and brightest producers to work with us, thus enhancing the network's chances of even more success. Beyond that, Marcy Carsey and Tom Werner achieved the status of hot properties and, upon the show's syndication in 1989, became rich beyond their wildest imaginings.

Cosby succeeded, I believe, because it was anything but the classic sitcom it appeared to be at first glance. It quickly developed its own unique look and texture, but it was never easy to accurately sum up in a few words what the series as a whole or any one of its episodes was about. Bill used to say, "I want people, when they watch this show, to say, 'Hey, how did they get those microphones and cameras into my house?'" In that, Cosby succeeded. In one sense, the show was simply about looking through the fourth wall of the Huxtable household. It was also, to a great degree, about the communicative powers of a man named Bill Cosby. And then of course it was about the thing that Cosby spent so much time communicating: real life.

The history of television can be seen as a series of Magic Moments—those small but brilliantly realized bits of TV business that allow everyone involved to breathe easier, knowing they have a success. Here's one of them:

The *Cosby Show* pilot contained a scene in which Dr. Huxtable goes into his son Theo's room to talk to him about his miserable report card. Did he really think someone with grades like this could get into college, Cliff asks his son. Theo, however, has another agenda. He's not going to college, he says. Just because his mother is a lawyer and his father is a doctor doesn't mean he has to be such an achiever—or so he tells his dad. Then Theo ends his little I-gotta-be-me speech by asking Cliff why a father can't accept and love his son simply for what he is.

The kid has stood his ground, and stated his position well. Everyone at the taping applauded wildly. Your standard sitcom would have stopped dead right there to bask in the audience reaction. Instead, after one or two beats, Cosby speaks up. He tells Theo that he's never heard anything so stupid—that being afraid to try is about the dumbest possible approach to life. His boy, Cliff says, is *going* to try. Why? Because I am your father and I say so, that's why.

The audience, having already applauded, could only cheer even louder. The cast, crew, and executives knew instantly that they had created something that worked.

A Magic Moment.

And—lest we forget—a 48 share in the overnights.

TWO

....

Okay, So Here's
the Pitch

"Now let me make sure I've got this straight," I say to the producer who is sitting across the desk from me. "What you're proposing here is . . . 'Noah's Ark: the Miniseries'?"

"Exactly!" he says. "You'll have this incredible boat, you'll have a flood right out of an Irwin Allen movie! You'll have the disaster freaks, you'll have the Bible Belters, and you'll pull in the kids' market, too—it'll be a goddamn forty share!"

"Gee," I say. "I really don't think so."

"Listen, Brandon, baby, you're not getting it. This is *Roots* with animals!"

Consider the pitch meeting.

For most of the eighties I probably had an average of six each day. I was pitched at 7:00 A.M. breakfasts and at the tail end of industry soirées, at a GE board meeting by former cabinet members, by a rabbi at my grandfather's funeral, and by my dentist during a root canal procedure (the procedure was less painful than the pitch). Given my longevity, I was probably on the receiving end of more pitches than Johnny Bench. It's scary to think that my brain may look like his knees.

And yet the classic pitch meetings—*Okay, here it is, Brandon, I know you're gonna love this*—remained a central part of my professional life. I never thought about eliminating them or even cutting back, and for one simple reason: I'm a very competitive person, and I wanted to make sure, in every way possible, that the next Kentucky-Derby-winner-of-a-TV-concept was not going to wind up in someone else's stable. In addition, the "pitchers" would have found me (or any executive with green-light power) anyway. It was as if I wore a homing device—they somehow knew how to pick up my scent in a crowded room.

I probably heard more than thirty thousand pitches during my fifteen years in TV programming. I once had a producer pitch me a *Mister Ed* reunion movie in which, he insisted, "this time the horse will speak only Italian." I had David Lynch, in his pre–*Twin Peaks* days, come in with an idea for a series about tadpolelike organisms called Lemeurians from the lost continent of Atlantis. Lynch is the kind of guy who can sit across the desk from you and chat about extraterrestrials and aliens as if he were talking about the Dodgers. "These beings have evolved to where they look exactly like humans," he explained. "The only way you can tell who they are is if you run an ad in a comic book that says, 'Draw the Pirate and Win a Five-Hundred-Dollar Art Scholarship.' These people always draw the two ears on the same side of the head."

My favorite pitch of all time? Easy: Marlon Brando.

I first heard that Brando was interested in doing a TV show from NBC senior vice president Steve Sohmer. "Brando is very eager to come in and talk about a project," Steve said. "Would you have time to take a meeting with him in the next week or two?"

"Is that, like, a trick question?" I said. "What's his number?"

So my office called his office, and one day I came in, looked in my appointment book, and there it was, on the line next to 3:00 P.M. that Friday: *the name.* I was so excited that at 2:55 on the appointed day I opened my door a crack and peeked out, thinking I might be imagining the whole thing. I wasn't. There was Brando, wearing a dark business suit, sitting on my couch in the waiting room and reading a back issue of *Time* magazine. He looked like a banker—a gigantic banker, yes, but a banker. Definitely not Stanley Kowalski or the Wild One. Definitely not Hollywood.

When he came in, he seemed a little nervous, though he was cool compared to me. I also sensed that, like the consummate actor he is, Brando had prepared for that afternoon's role as . . . the Businessman. The conservative clothes were part of that preparation, and so too was his smooth—but not too smooth—manner of speaking. He eased himself into a chair just across the desk from me and got to the point of his pitch in a way that showed me he was respectful of my time. And yet he never rushed the conversation, or behaved in a way that said, "Hey, I'm *Brando*, baby, and I've got better things to do." In fact, I was shocked, when it was over, to find that we'd talked for two and a half hours.

The show he wanted to do was definitely a special; in fact, it was somewhere out there beyond unique. "I've lived in Tahiti for quite a while," he began, "and I can tell you that the Polynesian culture is wonderful. The whole world would be a much better place if we all adopted the Polynesian culture. But you're probably trying to figure out what the hell is the show I'm talking about. . . ."

I shrugged meekly. He smiled and went on.

"Well, it's my home movies of Tahiti, of myself in the water, over a number of years, with all these beautiful native women. I've got thousands of minutes of this stuff. And I think I can get the Tahitian government to come in with me on the deal so the price won't be prohibitive. I think it would be a success. You put this thing on in February and it's fifteen below with the windchill factor, how can the guy in Pittsburgh *not* watch naked Tahitian women in the water and Marlon Brando when it comes on at ten P.M.?"

Ah, Marlon, Marlon! What a great job it would have been if I could have made decisions on the basis of emotional attachments to the people who pitched the ideas. *And what a great job it was!* The whole time he was talking about this rather impractical premise, I was nodding "Yes, *yes!*" and thinking, Hey, it's a relatively small expenditure, and I'm in business with *Marlon Brando.* Sounds good to me.

I never got a chance to actually say that, however, because Brando got himself sidetracked onto a discussion of his own rapid rise to fame. "One minute I was in New York delivering sandwiches to the New School," he said. "And the next I've got a part in a play. That led to another part, and then a year later I'm out here in Hollywood doing the movie version of *Streetcar Named Desire*."

I made the kind of observation at this point that will show you why I had the corner office. "That must have really been something," I said.

"For a year," Brando went on, "I never touched a door. I couldn't touch a door if I wanted to. People were opening them for me. I could show up at the fanciest restaurant at the busiest hour and they'd say, 'Right this way.' I'd sit up in my house in the Hollywood Hills getting bombed, and I'd be watching the news at ten P.M. and I'd see this blond woman doing the news and I'd call up the station. I'd ask to get her on the phone, and I'd say, 'Hi, sweetheart, this is Marlon Brando. I think you're real attractive. How'd you like to come over to my place when you're done?' And sure enough, she'd be over at my house about a half hour later, and I'd be in bed with her. It was just like ordering Chinese food. That was Hollywood, and it was great."

Then the conversation got . . . not strained, but a bit bumpy.

"So, Brandon, your name is like mine," he suddenly said.

"Yeah," I said. "Brando, Brandon."

"So who do you like in the Super Bowl?"

The game was that weekend—the Patriots versus the

....

Bears—and I told him that the Bears were obviously the favorite, but that we'd been the underdog network for so long I couldn't help rooting for the Patriots.

"Do you want to put some gelt on that?" he said.

And I melted in my chair. I don't know if this makes sense to a non–Brando fan. But to me that was the high point of the meeting, if not the week and the entire year: sitting there and hearing Brando—the personification of the era when hepness became hipness—use the word "gelt."

The rest of the meeting, in retrospect, was a bit of a bust, in the business sense. For one thing, we never were able to go forward with his special because he couldn't get the proper permissions from the Tahitian government. Second, Brando only gave me nine points when I took the Pats for five hundred dollars, instead of the thirteen points that were being listed as the line *in every newspaper in America.* (Not that I felt too bad about that. I would have lost anyway, and when the Godfather makes an offer . . .)

Third, I didn't, as I'd so fervently hoped, get the great one's autograph on the check I wrote him, which he deposited after the game turned out the way it did. Brando—in a very un-Brando-like move, if you ask me—endorsed it with a rubber stamp.

So what makes for a great pitch?

The first thing I look for is enthusiasm. If a person isn't passionate about an idea now, before he has written a word or set foot on a soundstage, what's going to happen five years from now, when the show is a hundred episodes old and staggering? William Paley used to have an expression: "Who's going to be worrying about this show at three o'clock in the morning?" If the person making the pitch isn't the answer to that question, you're in trouble.

The second quality is a connection to real life. If someone comes in and says, "You know, in 1964 I had an experience in summer camp that still haunts me," that person has got my attention. If the subject is a police action show, and Steve Cannell, the producer of *Hunter* and *The Commish,* starts waxing eloquent about how he spent three days hanging out with some guys who were in the Special Unit of the police force, and what great stories they told him—I'm sold already.

Another question I ask myself, as I listen to a pitch, is, How many stories can be spun out of this idea? All television is story-telling, and a successful show will need to spawn eighty to one hundred new stories in its lifetime. If there are only twelve great themes in Western literature, then I suppose there are only a finite amount of plots, true—but there are probably an infinite number of fresh perspectives. What the world doesn't need is the same stories that were on *Married with Children* and *Blossom* told all over again, except maybe not as well. Too often I would hear this kind of cannibalization in pitch meetings, and always by writers whose only reference was a successful show already on the air. When shows like these get produced—and they do—it's a classic example of the medium feeding on itself, and it's a big reason why television viewing today can sometimes seem like déjà-viewing.

Next, I think of the show in terms of actors' roles. The moment a pitch begins, a casting Rolodex whirls inside my mind, and I begin to think about what hot on-the-cusp actors can be matched with this show. I am a firm believer in the power of personalities to attract viewers. The simple dynamic of every hit show can be experienced in a question: Who are you waiting to have come through the door? If you, as the viewer, are not waiting for anyone in particular, the party's over. If you take a series like *Murphy Brown* and put in an actress of such class and dimension as Candice Bergen, you have a show of substance. You put an actor with Scott Bakula's range in *Quantum Leap,* and the series becomes not just viable but exciting to watch. You take a show like *Night Court,* put John Larroquette in the part of Dan Fielding, and you're on the air eight years. Besides, it's always a lot easier to develop a series when you know who it is you're writing for.

Say, the president.

Yes, I've even been pitched by the president of the United States. Sort of.

In 1980, a veteran Hollywood producer named A. C. Lyles, an elegant older gentleman who had been the best man at Ronald and Nancy Reagan's wedding, arrived in my office and said, "I've really got something great for you, and the president wants me to pitch it to you directly."

"The *president?*"

And then Lyles took out a typed-up treatment for a two-hour movie that would be four individual tales of Congressional Medal of Honor winners. "You get four great guest stars," he said. "The president will appear at the beginning and the end. You play it on Memorial or Veterans Day. It can't miss."

After he left, the first thing I noticed about the treatment was the way it smelled: musty. The onionskin paper had long since started moldering and turning yellow. I stopped short of doing any carbon dating, but my best guess was that the treatment had been left over from the early sixties. That was the period when *General Electric Theater* went off the air, and Reagan hadn't yet made his move into politics, and he was an out-of-work actor trying to get some action for himself. Clearly, he'd pulled this out of some trunk in the White House attic and given it to his old pal Lyles.

But how do you turn down the president of the United States? This was a tricky business indeed. Fred Silverman had once told me a story about something that happened in the early seventies when he was at CBS. They had a series at the time called *O'Hara, U.S. Treasury* starring David Janssen as a crime-fighting agent. The show was borderline in terms of the ratings, and while Silverman was considering whether to renew it for another season, he got a call from a guy at the Treasury Department who was serving as a liaison between the production company and the government. The man wanted to have a meeting, and so he came in from Washington and Fred took him to lunch.

"I understand that you're undecided about *O'Hara*," he told Fred. "You've gotta do what you've gotta do. But I just wanted to tell you that there are those of us down in Washington who like the idea of a weekly prime-time showcase. So if the show gets canceled, we're gonna do what *we've* gotta do."

Fred at the time assumed the guy was playing him. But the show was canceled, and about a dozen top CBS executives on both coasts had their income taxes audited the following year.

You can bet I had that in mind when I phoned Lyles and

told him we'd commissioned a script. Ultimately, though, the idea didn't work, and I couldn't bring myself to actually put it into production. We wound up giving the White House a consolation prize: a one-hour special called *Dear Mr. President,* in which we picked twelve kids who'd written letters to Reagan, and he took them on a tour of the U.S. Mint, the FBI Building, and other Washington high points.

It was while working on shows such as *Dear Mr. President* that I would sometimes stop what I was doing and scan my office to see where Allen Funt had hidden his camera.

For all their frequency, the protocol of pitch meetings is somewhat unformed. And there are no rules about who is too famous to do the pitching, though some people think showmanship is half the game.

Ray Stark, the producer of *Funny Girl, The Way We Were,* and several Neil Simon movies, once paid a call to my office. When I told him I was honored that he'd come to pitch an idea, he cut me off. "Thanks," he said. "But I have to make something clear. I don't pitch. I *am* the pitch." After that the meeting was pretty much a blur—mostly because I was singing "I Am the Walrus" to myself the whole time.

Pitches by nonhumans are fairly infrequent. I was once pitched a show by a chimpanzee (on videotape, so someone could do the voice-over; *Mr. Smith,* as it was called, lasted thirteen episodes) and on another occasion by a hand puppet (as you'll see). Usually, though, the someone peddling the project is an all-too-human independent producer angling for the standard thirteen- or twenty-two-episode commit-

ment. The pitch-person, however, might also be a writer, a
director, an actor, or a valet parker who hits you with six
concepts (any of which could be titled "The Incredible
Things That Happen to Valet Parkers") while you're waiting
for your car outside the Beverly Hills Hotel. I've even been
pitched shows by my own grandmother.

Jeanne Shapiro, my maternal grandmother, used to constantly write down ideas I should be pursuing and send me
the lists. One of her most persistent pitches was for a book she
had read, *Evergreen,* by Belva Plain. She had no vested interest in the property, of course—she was a doctor's wife living
in Palm Beach—but she was always saying, "Brandon, you
should get Barbra Streisand for this and make it into a miniseries."

"Grandma," I'd say, "Barbra Streisand doesn't do television. And besides, it's a Jewish story. There are only six million Jews. We're into large audiences here."

"So forget Streisand and get someone else," she said. "But
this is a love story that everyone will like."

When she was eighty-two, she got very sick and was on her
death bed. I flew down to Florida to visit her. Three minutes
into our conversation, she said, "Have you had any further
thoughts about *Evergreen?*"

After she died, I felt badly that I'd never done it and—
largely for sentimental reasons, I admit—I commissioned a
script of the book. Somewhat to my surprise, when the script
came in several months later, it was actually pretty good, and
I decided to begin production of a miniseries. In 1984 *Evergreen,* starring Lesley Ann Warren, became one of the key
pieces of programming in our February ratings sweeps. My

uncle Robert Shapiro—Grandma's son—happened to be in New York, as I was, at that time, and we had lunch together. I told him that I didn't really pray on a regular basis but that lately I had found myself praying that *Evergreen* did well. "Do you think Grandma, wherever she is, knows what's going on right now?" I asked him.

"Yes," he said. "And she's probably saying, 'I'm dead two years and the only time I hear from him is when he needs ratings.'"

In terms of ratings, by the way, *Evergreen* was a resounding success. In fact, it helped NBC win its first February sweeps week in years.

The problem with pitch meetings is that they are a low-percentage business; most of the ideas aren't as good as my grandmother's. You always start out brimming with hope and making a little industry conversation—and then as soon as the other guy starts telling you the concept that he swore on the phone would be bigger than *Cosby*, a combination of boredom and disappointment sweeps over you. Your eyes glaze; your heart sinks. Either you've heard it all before—or you've never heard such a ridiculous thing in your life. There are times, though, when the ridiculous can turn out to be the sublime.

Like the day when Bernie Brillstein came into my office with puppeteer/producer Paul Fusco. Paul was carrying a Hefty bag, out of which he pulled a furry little brown creature whose attitude was like a cross between Rodney Dangerfield and Groucho Marx. VP of comedy Perry Simon and I looked at each other as if Brillstein and Fusco had gone round the bend. The puppet instantly sneezed and proceeded to wipe his nose on my jacket sleeve. This little alien's name was ALF, and he made a world of difference to NBC.

On the other hand, Paul Mason, the coproducer of *Chico and the Man* and *Welcome Back, Kotter,* once came into my office in Burbank with four Native American would-be writers that he'd flown down from someplace in the Pacific Northwest. He was trying to sell me a sitcom set on a reservation and called *Life on the Res.* "This is going to be great," one of the women in the group said. "I want you to think of it as an Indian *Good Times.*"

Mason looked at me expectantly. "What do you think, Brandon?" he asked. "What I think," I said, "is that if the Indians are talking like this it's time to get out of the business."

Outwardly, the encounter between pitch-person and TV executive resembles a call paid by an office-copier sales representative. And yet there is no product to wheel in, no catalog to show. All the pitch-person has to offer is an idea, and that requires two different people to use their imaginations. As a result, the question of exactly what the product *is* can sometimes be open to debate. Maybe a movie-of-the-week is being pitched, but the executive thinks it has possibilities as a series. Maybe the characters are great but are in the wrong setting.

I remember reading in *Esquire* Garry Marshall's idea for what to do to cover the soft spot of a pitch: Pepper it with swear words. Just raise your voice, and curse your way through it. *So the cop comes through the f—ing door and sees the f—ing perp by the bar and he punches him in the f—ing face and he falls down on the goddamn floor and he gives it to him right there.*

But most pitches aren't that robust. Too many of them consist of a middle-aged producer telling you that his new twenty-six-year-old wife really gets along well with his twenty-three-year-old daughter from his first marriage. They're like sisters—no, best friends!—he says. And he thinks he could develop the concept into a successful sitcom. What that producer doesn't realize, though, is that 60 percent of sitcom viewers are women. And the show he has just described—twentysomething female steals away not just the husband but *the daughter, too*—is many women's worst nightmare. So it's a super idea, yes, if you're trying to alienate half the population.

Like some movies and TV shows, some pitches are so bad that they are entertaining on a level that was never intended. Sherwood Schwartz, the creator of *Gilligan's Island* and *The Brady Bunch,* came to see me once around the time that ABC did *The Day After,* a riveting made-for-television movie about a nuclear holocaust. He was very excited. NBC had done a *Gilligan's Island* reunion movie with him, and we'd gotten a huge 53 share, and now Schwartz came in with a seven-page presentation that attempted to tie together those two big concepts. It was called, not surprisingly, *Gilligan's Island: The Day After.*

The idea was that the people on the island hear a radio report that says nuclear bombs are going off and the world will end in twenty-four hours. So they panic, because if the world is ending, who's going to carry on? So several people, including Gilligan and Ginger, decide to get married to repopulate the world. The second hour turned into *The Blue Lagoon,* with the second generation of Gilligan's Islanders falling in love and discovering their sexuality. Ultimately, they learn from a guy on a fishing boat that the broadcast about the nuclear bomb was just a *War of the Worlds*–type hoax. Everyone else on the planet realized that fifteen years before, but the islanders' radio batteries had gone dead immediately following the announcement, so they'd never heard that it was just a big joke.

When Schwartz finished telling me this, I put down his proposal and stared at him with genuine awe. "Sherwood," I said, "you've done the impossible. You've taken two fifty-share movies—a *Gilligan's Island* reunion and *The Day After*—put them together, and created a twenty-five share movie."

A common characteristic of the people who think up things like this is that they can't wait to tell them to you. When they call and ask for a meeting, they sound as if an idea is burning a hole in their brain. And if you can't see them right away, or have to cancel, they get apoplectic. When I was at ABC in the mid-seventies, my boss, the late Steve Gentry, was unexpectedly called away one day, just before he was to receive a pitch from a producer named Mark Carliner. I apologized to Carliner—whose claim to fame at that time was *Flying High,* a show about the adventures of three female flight attendants—and told him that Steve had asked me to fill in and hear his idea. Carliner had only one question: Did

I have the authority to give him a go-ahead if I liked what I heard? When I told him, Actually, no, Mark, I don't, he exploded.

"This guy has owed me a meeting for five weeks," he screamed. "I'm not taking this crap anymore. He promised me a script." Then he went behind Gentry's desk, took his chair, and began wheeling it down the hallway. If he didn't get a meeting, and quickly, Carliner said, we would never see that piece of office furniture again.

He got his meeting, so the tactic worked. The pitch, however, didn't.

Steve Gentry, by the way, once gave me some very good Words to Live By. "Every producer has a fifteen-share show inside him," he said. "It's our job to keep it inside him. They all want to do Ionesco. *Don't let them do Ionesco.*"

Since a network usually buys only about a hundred scripts a year for all of its series pilots, the odds are more than 20–1 against the person making the pitch. A good number seem to sense what they are up against, and they try in various ways to stand out from the crowd. After all, a lot is at stake. Pots of gold wait at the end of the rainbow for any producer who has a hit that goes the distance. One hundred episodes. The Hollywood dream. "Fuck You" money. But most of them would settle for an order, any order, to get into the game, to get to another season. To have at least "Goddamn You" money. *The Cosby Show* earned something like $500 million during its initial cycle of syndication, largely because it was exactly what the market wanted—a good half-hour sitcom. In addition, *The Cosby Show* spearheaded the onslaught of eighties comedies—*Full House, Married with Children, Murphy*

Brown—that the increasingly competitive independent stations so fervently craved.

However, that kind of sheer wealth is too distant for most
pitch-people to consider. What's usually motivating them,
besides visions of more moderate, short-term financial gain,
is the chance to have their ideas validated—*I love it; I'll give
you thirteen episodes!*—and then beamed into millions of
American homes.

Robert Blake, known for *Baretta* and his performance in *In
Cold Blood,* is an example of someone who formulates a theory about what the TV audience wants, builds a TV show
around that theory, and then becomes passionate about con-
vincing you to agree with him.

Blake burst into my office one day dressed as a priest. "Who
is the biggest hit of all time?" he said.

"Uh, I don't know, Bob—*Sixty Minutes?*" I said. *"Walt
Disney?"*

I was willing to play along with him because, although
Blake can be hard to deal with on the set, I kind of liked the
way his flakey, maverick mind works.

"Okay, Bob. I give up," I said. "Who's the biggest hit of all
time? Tell me."

"It's Jesus Christ," Blake said. "He was born two thousand
years ago, and he's bigger today than when he was alive. He's
the biggest hit in history, and what I want to do is give you
Jesus Christ in East L.A." The show he was pitching was called
Hell Town, the story of a barrio-based Catholic priest.

Blake was right as far as the pilot episode went. It ran on
March 6, 1985, against the top-ten hit *Dynasty,* and NBC
achieved its best rating of the season in that time slot. The

subsequent series, though, lasted only seventeen weeks—but, to use some biblical parlance, it seemed like an eternity.

Michael Landon was a whole other story conference. When he talked about a show, he was as serious and as focused as Blake, but much more calm and self-assured. Once, when *Little House on the Prairie* was in its ninth season, he dropped in to discuss his next project. We began by talking about our favorite movies, and he mentioned *It's a Wonderful Life.* "That's one of my favorites, too," I told him.

"I'm glad," he said, "because I'd like to do something with the same spirit, the same human values. I'd like to play an angel of God who comes down each week and changes somebody's life, just like Clarence did for Jimmy Stewart. I mean, wouldn't you like to believe that there's someone out there who can intercede on your behalf and straighten things out with your stepfather, your mother, your children, or your boss at work?"

"Michael," I said, "you're going to write, produce, direct, and star in a series where you essentially play God. No pun intended, but you're going to get crucified by the TV critics."

Landon let that one slide. "I'm a big boy. I've been on television every week for over twenty years. I can take my licks," he said. "Critics don't bother me. All I know is that a lot of people come into your office and say, 'I know how to make people laugh.' And I know you guys are very big on sitcoms. But I do something else that's just as powerful, but much more rare. I know how to make people cry. And I believe that there's an audience for that. If you can move people in an hour of television, they'll be back next week for more."

"Okay," I said, "go off and write it."

And write he did. Michael was back in a week with a two-hour, first-draft pilot script. His working title at the time was *Jonathan Smith*. I jokingly referred to the show as "Jesus of Malibu," and then, when Landon reminded me that he was Jewish, "Moses of Malibu." The actual name for the show was lifted from a project that was as far from Landon's deeply felt, humanistic show as you could imagine—a remake of *Route 66* with two stunningly attractive women driving around America in a sports car. "Why don't we call your show *Highway to Heaven?*" I asked Landon. He considered that for a couple of seconds and said, "Yeah, sure." That, it turned out, was the sum total of NBC's contribution to Landon's heartwarming success.

Highway to Heaven is an example of an idea that I personally thought was preposterous but had no intention of derailing, at least not immediately. For one thing, we had a commitment to do another series with Landon. But I respected Landon's talent, even if he made the kind of shows that I myself would probably never view on a regular basis. Besides, every time I looked at him, I heard the *Bonanza* theme in my head. I simply couldn't say, "Sorry, what else have you got?" to Little Joe.

Highway turned out to be the kind of show that tested my faith. When the script was read, a lot of people at NBC, myself included, thought it was a trifle old-fashioned. And when Landon did a rough-cut screening of the pilot, Jeff Sa-

gansky—who was at the time my number-one son/chief lieutenant—was severely disappointed.

"This show is so dated," he said, "they should have shot it
in black-and-white. It's an embarrassment. I don't even think
we should show it at our management screening."

"Jeff, we're spending three million dollars on this thing,"
I said. "We've got to put it up there."

"But it's so slow. It'll empty the screening room."

"Give me a cassette for the weekend."

I was going to San Francisco to visit my parents for Pass-
over. Lilly's family came with us. At about five o'clock, I put
on the cassette in the living room, and Lilly's father came in.
At six o'clock we were called to dinner. I got up; he stayed.
"Where's Jack?" everyone was saying. That was my first indica-
tion that we jaded TV executives might not be the best judges
of Landon's show.

Sagansky was right about the management screening.
There were forty people in the room when it started, and only
about fifteen at the end. The advertisers' screenings in New
York and Chicago went about the same way. Some ad people
in the audience were laughing derisively. "I know we have a
series commitment," people kept saying to me. "But let's just
cut our losses and not put it on the air."

In the end, there was only one group of people who loved
Highway, and they were a rather large segment of the American viewing audience. The same two-hour pilot that the TV
pros had scoffed at opened with a 37 share and built every
half hour that night. It wound up beating *The Fall Guy*, an
ABC show that had been a top-ten hit, in its 8:00 P.M.
Wednesday time slot. Its first year on the air was also the first

time in thirty years that NBC was number one in the ratings. Yes, Jonathan Smith helped a lot of people learn to believe.

The final thing I look for in a pitch—almost always in vain—is an original idea, a concept so special and different that even a grizzled veteran of pitch meetings like me has never heard it before. Just the promise of one of those can get my heart beating quickly. And you never know when you're going to hear one.

That, in any case, is the only excuse I can think of for leaving the office in the middle of a busy day back in 1979 to hear a major film producer—a man with several monster hits to his credit (who shall remain nameless)—suggest a show. I should have known better—but then again, if someone ever opens a Museum of the Pitch, I've already got something they can hang in the main hall.

The producer wanted me to come to his bungalow on his studio lot to hear about a weekly series in which, I was told, he would work both in front of and behind the camera. His unofficial intermediary, a powerful executive in his own right, had come by to extend the invitation, and kept insisting that the trip would be time well spent. After all, this producer was not exactly some fly-by-night type operating out of a phone booth on Melrose Avenue.

What I remember most about the man's office is that it was dark—and that there were so many pictures on the wall of him with various celebrities, I felt like I was in a seedy Italian restaurant. He himself was sitting smack-dab in the middle of all the dimness in a high-backed, red leather chair, wearing sunglasses.

"I've been told you TV guys like something to be pitched to you in one sentence," he said as soon as I sat down, "so maybe I should just cut to the chase."

"Well," I said, "I'm ready."

"Okay. Here it goes, and it is just one sentence."

He paused. And what he said to me (I swear) was this: "A woman's pubic hair is stronger than the transatlantic cable."

There was another pause. A long one. I looked across the room. The emissary was nodding as if he had heard some timeless truism like "It's not what you know, it's who you know."

Then the producer said, "Brandon, you look like you don't understand what I just told you."

I said I understood every syllable, but that I didn't see how it translated into a weekly TV series.

"Hey," he said, leaning in now, "I'm talking about love stories, man. I'm talking about grabbing women by the crotch and not letting them go until fifty-two minutes later. I'll open the show and close the show, just like Alfred Hitchcock. The world wants a new love story. I'll give them one every week. I'll steam up your screen."

Usually, when a person is making a pitch, I'm asking myself, Where will this fit on the schedule? Can it solve my problem on Friday night? Will it make a good lead-in to the eleven o'clock news? Is this idea so good that I should say yes even if I don't have a place on the schedule for it, just so I can keep it away from my competitors? Now, however, I had a different question:

How do I get from *this* couch to *that* door? Beam me up, Scotty.

My mind raced for something pseudoprofessional to say.

"Gee," I finally said to him, "that's an anthology. We just did a couple of anthologies, and Fred Silverman is really down on them. After our *Supertrain* experience I don't think we want to rush back on those tracks again."

I didn't have much to say on the ride back. Not that the producer's emissary seemed to notice. As we pulled into the NBC lot, he smiled wide and said, "See, I told you it would be worth the drive."

THREE

....

My Year of
Living Dangerously

There are several kinds of
silence.

There is, for example, the powerful kind you hear at night
in the forest; the sudden and sorry kind you hear at a baseball
game when a player from the visiting team hits a home run.
Then there's the kind I heard one day in 1982 as I stood
before the twelve angry men who constituted NBC's tough,
highly influential affiliate board. That silence was the sicken-
ing kind. The kind that comes when your job is on the line
and you've just made a presentation of your fall lineup and
all you hear is the sound of one hand clapping.

Not my favorite kind of silence at all.

No one's life is a sitcom. My life, in fact, has at times more closely resembled an overly dramatic made-for-television movie. In 1982, I hit bottom—professionally, emotionally, and, certainly, physically. NBC's ratings were so low that there were days when, after calling New York for the over-nights at 7:00 A.M. California time, I would almost be too depressed to go to work. I had a real connection to those shows, and so I took their failure personally. It's bad enough to be rejected by your friends, your wife, or your family; I felt like I was being rejected by *an entire nation*.

When I did drag myself into the office, people would tell me how horrible I looked. Then they'd hit me with that old industry cliché: "Hey, Brandon, you gotta lighten up. This is just television, you know. We're not curing cancer here."

That didn't strike me as funny, and for a good reason. In addition to all my programming problems, I *had* cancer—a fairly serious recurrence of Hodgkin's disease, a cancer of the lymphatic system that requires heavy-duty chemotherapy. I've never acknowledged this publicly until now. At the time, only Lilly, a few close friends, my parents, and my boss, Grant Tinker, knew. But from speaking to cancer patients one-on-one and in groups, I've since seen the good that can come from sharing stories about the disease. It's reassuring to know that other people have had the same fear you do, and to see that it's possible to overcome not only the fear and the ex-treme discomfort of the treatment, but also the cancer itself.

Back then, however, rumors about me circulated around town, some of them true, some not. Yes, that was a wig on my head; my hair had fallen out from the chemo. And no, I wasn't "living on borrowed time"—I was, rather, living a life punctuated by weekly treatments. Friday afternoon would find me at the UCLA Medical Center reading scripts while a powerful chemical dripped into my veins. The treatment started on August 5, 1982, and ended exactly 365 days later.

My year of living dangerously.

Back to the affiliate board meeting, definitely one of my darker moments.

"Jesus Christ, Brandon," says a rep from the South as he gets settled in his seat for my preview of the coming season. *"Cheers* is a sixteen share, and you've just bought nine more episodes?"

"Maybe *Cheers* is a sixteen share in your town," says another rep from the Midwest. "Where I come from it's a nine."

"Shelley Long has got some genuine talent," adds yet another. "But that Ted Danson is a stiff. His hair looks weird."

Quite a joy, these annual gatherings. A dozen representatives of the network's two hundred plus affiliated stations travel (at the network's expense) to some exotic locale (in this case, the La Quinta Resort in Palm Springs) to question the competence of NBC's executives, the merit of our programs, and the wisdom of our competitive strategy. The network encourages this kind of behavior because without the affiliates there would *be* no network. Imagine a car company without car dealers, or a shoe manufacturer without shoe stores. The affiliates form a nationwide distribution system, a way to get the shows—and the commercials within them—to the viewers. So important is this partnership that the networks pay the affiliates a fee just for carrying their programs. In addition, the affiliates are compensated by receiving free commercial time during network programs—time that they can, in turn, sell to local advertisers.

The affiliates are also a network's main line to what our business calls the "flyover people"—people who live in between New York and L.A. The real television audience: the heartland of our country. The affiliates can tell you what their local audience really feels about your shows. Not what the critics feel, but how people in their living rooms are really responding to what you're putting on the air. In this way the affiliates are like members of Congress; they let the networks know—loud and clear—what their constituency likes and doesn't like. Usually, they feel, the networks never get it quite right, so these broadcasters from Portland, Oregon, to Portland, Maine, are always lobbying to modify or replace your programs—especially during the affiliates' annual summer meeting (where those two hundred plus men and women don't hold back what's on their minds) and at the even tougher affiliate board meetings.

And network executives do want to keep the affiliates happy. Because if the affiliates aren't happy, the network has problems. The first sign of trouble is when your local stations decide to preempt your shows, thereby diminishing their chances of success; after that the relationship could deteriorate to the point where they defect to one of your rivals and take their audience with them. And when your viewers decline in number, the rates you charge for your national advertising decline as well. That's a fairly effective club to brandish over a network's head, and the affiliates often brandish it with gusto.

In '82, they were edgier than ever. To be honest, they had

reason to be. NBC was then starting its seventh straight season in last place—a situation that depressed *everybody's* psyche, not to mention ad revenues. By then the affiliates had been given almost a decade's worth of empty promises. They'd been given Fred Silverman as the Messiah, and then, just two months before this board meeting, they'd been given Grant Tinker as . . . well, what do you call someone who tries to salvage things after a Messiah fails to deliver? And the final thing they'd been given was me. At the age of thirty-three, I'd been running the entertainment division for two years, and while I was proud of some of the shows in our lineup, we'd made almost no measurable ratings improvement.

"This is not a situation we can turn around overnight," Grant had told the affiliates the day before. "I know you don't want to hear this, but you're going to need patience."

He was right about everything, especially about them not wanting to hear it.

"St. Elsewhere *is a festival of depression each week. Don't your writers know any medical stories where the patients get well?*"

"Knight Rider *slipped in the ratings last week. You're probably too young, but some of us remember* My Mother the Car *on NBC. I hope you've got a replacement standing by.*"

"*I just don't get this* Remington Steele. *It's a poor man's* Hart to Hart *with no star power. Why are we always copying the competition?*"

I didn't have the wherewithal to remind them that *Hart to Hart* was a poor man's *McMillan and Wife,* an NBC show. I didn't have the credibility to assure them that these were all well-made shows and would eventually stick with the audience.

So, in an attempt to appease the board members, I put on a ten-minute clip from *The A-Team,* a series that would premiere in January. I was extremely proud of the show, which I viewed as a superbly crafted, state-of-the-art action-adventure hour. In the years since, many people have tried and, it seems, failed to re-create the mix of action, adventure, character, and broad comedy that Steve Cannell and coexecutive producer Frank Lupo brought to *The A-Team.* Today, the genre seems to have graduated to the big screen, where films like *Lethal Weapon* and *Batman* make hundreds of millions of dollars and hold the mass moviegoing audience in thrall. But, in that meeting room in 1982, *The A-Team* did not exactly draw a chorus of bravos. I was looking for it to appease the board members, and it did—if you can call grown men rolling their eyes heavenward appeased.

In retrospect, I can see why showing scenes of a wildly dressed, crazily coiffed black man named Mr. T to a bunch of rock-ribbed Republican affiliate reps might not result in instant salvation. All I can say is, it seemed like a good idea at the time. The clip in question had T bursting heroically into a Wild West–type saloon where a seven-foot Mexican was terrorizing the local citizens. The way the sequence starts, you expect T to wipe the floor with the villain. But in a rather neat twist that sets up a later confrontation, the bad guy rears up and kicks T's butt back into the street.

When the lights came on, and the conversation didn't, I knew I was in trouble. In about four months, *The A-Team* would be the number-one show in America, surpassing *60 Minutes.* But to those affiliate reps, this was just further proof of what they had already been thinking: that I was in way over my head. Their silence was finally broken by the low din of the board members conferring in hushed tones with Grant Tinker and some of the other NBC people in the room. Finally, Ray Timothy, then head of Affiliate Relations, got up, walked over to me, and said, "Brandon, the board would like you to leave the room. They have a situation they'd like to talk about in a smaller group."

Thrown out of my own meeting. Great.

It was raining in the desert that day.

That was the first thing I noticed as I stared through the glass-paneled walls of the lobby. The lobby was the only place I could think of to go while my destiny was being debated. I'd already checked out of my room, and my bags were waiting. If Grant or anybody else came out of that meeting and said that he wanted to lessen my responsibilities, or fire me, I figured I'd just pack up my car and put some miles between me and the shards of my NBC career.

The second thing I noticed, from my reflection in the glass, was that my wig was curling up at the sides. Lilly had helped me put it on every morning—but she was eight and a half months pregnant with Calla and couldn't make this trip. I smoothed down the hairpiece as best I could. Then I stared out at the storm and, as many people are apt to in moments of crisis, I thought back on the events that had led me to this crossroads. Was I being ungrateful? Was the affiliate board right? Had I gotten too much too soon? I'd had something of a meteoric rise at NBC—two quantum-leap promotions in four years. But when you're on such a fast track it's hard to control the momentum, to confront the fact that you might be back at square one, in your beat-up, rusted-out Toyota, newly arrived in L.A.

As you might imagine, I didn't suddenly lose my ambition after I got my first network job at ABC. In fact, I stayed there only about a year. Working as director of current dramatic series with Fred Silverman while he was at ABC had been great; every time I dealt with him, I learned at the master's feet. My basic problem with the job was that I didn't interact with Fred enough. Often he was three thousand miles away at the executive offices in New York. He was also separated from me, in the corporate sense, by several layers of executives—and not just the usual bunch of network suits, either. Fred had surrounded himself with an all-star team featuring Michael Eisner (now the chairman and CEO of Walt Disney), Brandon Stoddard (who went on to run the ABC network and then preside over ABC Productions), Tom Werner and Marcy Carsey (who would go on to produce *The Cosby Show*), and Len Hill (one of the leading producers of television movies). I felt like a third-string quarterback on a Super Bowl–bound team. Maybe, I thought to myself after my year there was winding down, it's time to move on and get some playing time.

Serendipity has always played a large role in my life. This time it took the form of a timely phone call in August 1977 from Dick Ebersol, then the vice president of comedy and variety programs at NBC. A couple of years before, I'd come to New York and shown Dick my résumé tape of locally produced comedy sketches in hope of landing a writing job on *Saturday Night Live*. Now, though, he was calling about an opening NBC had for a position called director, comedy programs. That sounded impressive—unless you knew that "comedy programs" at Dick's network consisted of just two shows: *Sanford and Son* and *Chico and the Man.* Or at least that's what they were called the previous season. In the interim, Freddie Prinze, the star of *Chico,* had committed suicide; Redd Foxx, who played Fred Sanford, had quit his show to go to ABC; and Demond Wilson, who played his son, had pulled a gun on Norman Lear and Norman showed him the American Way to the door.

"I don't want to mislead you, Brandon," Dick said. "All we really have left at the moment is *The Man* and the sets from *Sanford.*"

I told Dick that I'd think about it.

What finally made up my mind to go to NBC were two words that an executive at ABC spoke to me late one afternoon while bribing me with some miniseries projects he would add to my plate if I stayed. The words were "David Eisenhower."

Let me digress.

Flashback to my freshman year at Yale. While flipping through a copy of *Time* magazine, I see a picture of Julie Nixon, then a student at Smith, and I bet my roommate twenty-five dollars that I can convince her to go out with me. Even though I am but a mere freshman, I write a letter that is at the very least, "sophomoric." It would make Cyrano green with envy. I pour my heart out. I drop the note in the mail. Nothing happens. Then I send another letter. I tell her how miserable I feel about her silence (yes, alas, it's a recurring theme). A few days later, I actually do get a reply—from

Julie Nixon's then new beau, David Eisenhower. To add insult to injury, the letter has been signed by about twenty of his dorm buddies at Amherst. "Please keep writing, Brandon," it says, "we all find your letters a scream. But give us a month in between epistles. We need a chance to recover." I pay my roommate the twenty-five dollars and lick my wounds . . .

. . . until about a year later, when I go to a mixer at Mount Holyoke, lose my ride back, and wind up crashing in a high school friend's dorm room nearby at Amherst. "A lot of my roommates are gone for the weekend," my friend says. "Just grab any empty bed." I do, and when I wake up, I see, from the names written on some textbooks, that the room I have grabbed belongs to David Eisenhower. I cannot let this opportunity pass. "Dear David," I write. "Glad that I finally got to sleep in the same bed as Julie Nixon—Love, Brandon." I pin the note to his pillow.

End of flashback.

Now we are back at ABC, and the executive is saying to me, "We're going to be doing a miniseries about Ike, and I'd like you to deal with the representative of the family. That would be his grandson David."

I envisioned several possible scenarios for how this was going to work out—all of them embarrassing. If I'd had to, I'm sure I could have gone through with it. I suppose I could have leveraged my way to the director of miniseries job at ABC—and been out of it two weeks later when David Eisenhower told my boss that he just couldn't work with me. But I didn't have to do that. I could go to NBC—and not have anyone think I was a potential John Hinckley in the making.

• • •

I almost quit there after about a year, too. The network was already in last place at that point, and it was all too easy to see why. I started the job in September 1977, and by January I'd pulled together the best writers, producers, actors, and writers—not that money could buy, but who would work at NBC. I'd overseen the making of twelve pilots, and I was proud of them. When Paul Klein, the head of programming, and Robert Mulholland, the head of the network, came out of the screening room and told me they were the best comedy pilots they'd ever seen, I was delighted. But when the final schedule was announced and only two of my shows appeared there— *The Waverly Wonders* with Joe Namath, and Garry Marshall's *Who's Watching the Kids*—I was disappointed and disgusted enough to think about quitting. Then the phone rang, and it was Fred Silverman calling. "I just want to tell you that I've just announced I'm coming over there," he said. "I heard you're unhappy, but sit tight, because everything's going to change around there, and you're going to be a big part of it."

I wasn't surprised. NBC had to do *something* to show its stockholders and affiliates that it was trying to turn things around. And Fred, the man who had brought CBS and ABC from last to first, the man who had been hailed on the cover of *Time* as "the Man with the Golden Gut," was an inspired hire. Of course, not everyone loved Fred. A few months earlier, Richard Reeves had written a piece in *Esquire* in which he said Fred had "brilliantly and cynically manipulated [the] system, testing . . . national standards or just apathy with prostitute entertainment and thug adventure." Reeves got it all wrong, though. What Fred wanted to do most of all was win the TV game. And there was nothing cynical about him.

Fred was one of the few people I've ever known who laughed where the laugh track laughed and got misty watching a daytime soap opera. He truly loved television.

Fred certainly was right about one thing: Things weren't going to be the same at NBC. They were about to get much worse. A sense of panic set in, and Fred began to scream, pound his desk, and threaten to fire senior executives on a regular basis. One time I was speaking at an industry luncheon in Hollywood when someone from the floor asked me, "Mr. Tartikoff, is it true no one at NBC can make the slightest move without first consulting Fred Silverman?"

With my best Jack Benny pause I replied, "I'll have to get back to you on that."

One of Fred's worst meltdowns came when we were working on *The Neighborhood*. The show was set in blue-collar Queens, New York. We had brought in Jimmy Breslin, the ultimate Queens Guy, to write the show's bible, a fifty-page outline that would describe the characters and the setting. The show had a marvelous plot, too, about block busting in an Archie Bunker–type neighborhood—sort of an Americanized version of the classic long-running British series *Coronation Street*. We made an excellent pilot starring Howard Rollins, Ben Masters, and Michael Gross. And then, feeling good about the project, I shipped the two three-quarter-inch cassettes off to New York so Fred and the East Coast contingent could see them.

At six-thirty California time the next evening, the Mickey Mouse phone that I had hooked up to serve as a "hot line" to Fred's New York office started ringing. "Either this is a wrong number," I said to myself, "or Fred is working late."

The voice on the phone was Ray Timothy's. His tone was stern. "Brandon, I'm here with Fred, and we have a problem. I've never seen him quite like this."

I heard Fred in the background screaming. Next there was a pause while he wrested the receiver from Ray's hands. "How many projects are you going to fuck up?" he said. "We had a brilliant script on *The Neighborhood*. But Ray and I just started watching it, and what I want to know is, who is the genius who decided to bring the black people into the beginning of the show? Who *are* these characters? None of it's set up. If this was one of your bright ideas, your ass is gone!"

He slammed the phone down on the desk. A second later, Timothy picked it up. I spoke first.

"Ray," I said, "please go to the tape deck, eject the cassette, and bring it back with you to the phone."

When he returned, I said, "Now read me what it says on the label."

"It says, '*The Neighborhood*, Part Two.' "

"Okay, now go and tell Fred that you've been watching the cassettes in the wrong order."

If you've never heard of *The Neighborhood* that may be because of this story. The show never made it onto the NBC schedule.

Fred's way of working himself out of the hole was to be a riverboat gambler: He decided to put on James Clavell's epic *Shōgun* in the form of an elaborate, twelve-part miniseries starring Richard Chamberlain as Blackthorne, an American seaman marooned in nineteenth-century Japan. *Shōgun* was the story of a stranger in a strange land, and from the start Clavell insisted that the Japanese characters speak their lines in *Japanese* with no English subtitles. That way, the audience could experience this world exactly the way Blackthorne experienced it. Here was a risky move for network TV, but Fred went along. At least initially. As we got closer to the air date, however, he began to waver. "Why can't we help the viewers out a little here?" he would say. "How about putting up a little legend on the screen every four or five minutes explaining what's going on?"

It became my job to carry that message to Clavell. Throughout that summer, I made several visits to the author to reiterate that while we respected the artistic integrity of his novel, the network had made a considerable investment, and our research suggested that the American television audience might not be willing to decipher the intent of the Japanese language. And all summer, Clavell would hold his position: "Do you have a firm air date yet? I've got a deal with Safeway to have *Shōgun* by the checkout counters in seventeen hundred stores. I need to give them a firm air date." In the end, we held to Clavell's vision.

After a few months of this, I needed a vacation, and so I escaped to Paris to see my then girlfriend and now wife, Lilly. She was a dancer with the New York City Ballet, which was then on the last leg of a European tour. I had met her two years before, at a tennis party at a friend's house in L.A. We were from completely different worlds; since the age of seven, Lilly had been spending ten hours a day, six days a week, practicing and performing ballet. She didn't watch TV or care a thing about show business (I felt the same way about ballet), and I found that very refreshing. For the first six months we knew each other, we were just friends, and that's probably one reason why our relationship has endured. We both knew what we were getting into.

A few days after I arrived in Paris, *Shōgun* premiered. "Aren't you going to call in?" Lilly said. "I mean, you *always* call for the ratings."

"You know, Lilly," I said, trying to affect a kind of French fatalism, "it's either going to succeed or fail. And there's nothing I can do about it here. If it's big news one way or the other, I'll read about it in the *International Herald Tribune.*"

Give me credit: I was *trying* to believe what I was saying. But by the next week, when Lilly and I were in Rome, I simply *had* to find out how the show was doing. I walked the streets until I found a kiosk on the Via Veneto that sold weekly *Variety*. With Lilly at my side, I turned to the television section—and saw a headline that said something like NBC HAS GREAT WEEK—*SHŌGUN* THIRD-HIGHEST-RATED MINISERIES OF ALL TIME.

"Oh, God," I couldn't help saying. "Here I am hanging around Rome and Paris during the one week it would have been great to be at NBC."

Lilly just let that one go by. Like I said, she knew what she was getting into.

I can tell you the exact moment that I knew my job was going to be the biggest uphill battle since Sisyphus'. It was on the very day I was named president of the entertainment division. NBC threw me a big party at the broadcast center in Burbank. They've got helium balloons, they've got jug wine, they've got Mylar streamers hanging from the walls—and this is the network that David Letterman calls cheap. Among the celebrities in attendance are the stars of several upcoming NBC shows.

Most of these people I already know. But the stars of one
show are complete strangers to me and, as it will turn out, to
the rest of America as well. *Pink Lady and Jeff* is a new variety
show, and since variety shows are handled out of New York,
I decide to go over and introduce myself to the cast. The
"Jeff" in the title is Jeff Altman, one of the better stand-up
comedians around. Then I walk over to the two Japanese
women known as Pink Lady. "Hi, I'm Brandon Tartikoff," I
say, "and I'm looking forward to working with you." They
look at me with frozen smiles, then run to get their manager,
who says, "Brandon, you'll have to excuse us, but the girls
don't speak English yet."

I remember standing there and thinking, We're a nation of
two-hundred-fifty million people. There's only one variety
show on all of network television. And we've selected two
hosts who don't speak English as their native tongue. Who's
going to sponsor this? Berlitz?

Pink Lady and Jeff would live for exactly six weeks, but
gained immortality as a recurring punch line in Carson
monologues for years to come.

Despite the swirling chaos endemic to NBC, I had never even
considered the fact that I might someday be in jeopardy of
losing my job.

Slow dissolve to the La Quinta lobby.

I am still watching it rain when the meeting-room door
suddenly swings open and everyone starts streaming out in
the direction of the dining room. Ray Timothy spots me and
takes me aside. "You should know," he says, "that they went
after you. They think you have too much in your hands. They

want to split daytime off from your division and give it to somebody else."

I feel the anger rise and struggle to keep my composure.

"So what happened?"

"Tinker didn't want to do that. He thought you were capable. He said he'd work with you to get a strong head of daytime, but he didn't want to take anything away from you."

This didn't surprise me. Practically from the moment he'd arrived at NBC four months earlier, Grant Tinker had been gracious and generous in the way he handled power. In moments of crisis, he was calm. Not the calm before the storm, because with Grant there rarely was a storm. Like Fred, he had a brilliant perspective on programming and the people charged with creating it. I remember one day just a few weeks after he'd come over from his highly successful MTM Productions, and all hell seemed to break loose at NBC. We had all barely adjusted to the news that James Garner, who had fallen off a horse and sustained a painful injury while shooting *Bret Maverick,* would be out for several months and the series would have to be shut down. Then came word that Rock Hudson, who was starring in *The Devlin Connection,* had to be taken to the hospital for emergency heart-bypass surgery. I called Grant, conditioned to expect that he would bark out orders, scramble the program schedule, and invoke passages from the Book of Job. But his voice, as always, was serene; his tone, trustful.

"So, Brandon," he said quietly, "what do you think we should do?" Grant wasn't dumping the responsibility on me, he was seeking advice from someone who'd survived a lot of harrowing experiences at that network. This was both an unsettling and an exhilarating moment. Unsettling because it had been a long time between sips, getting asked what *I* thought we should be doing. And consequently, so exhilarating that I worked all that weekend and the next five years of weekends to make Grant Tinker look prescient simply because he had asked.

Cancer helps you see things more clearly. The disease, I've found, can actually *help* you do your job, and there's a very simple reason why: There's nothing like cancer to keep you focused on what's important.

During my year of living dangerously I learned to invest my energy wisely. Lilly was always amazed when I came home fuming about how the production schedule on my favorite project was being derailed by the weather, or how a certain star had walked off a show. She never understood why I couldn't let go. "There are so many shows and so many fragile egos," she used to say. "When are you just going to accept that and stop letting it eat you up?" When I was coping with cancer, I finally did. Fighting an illness can set your priorities straight. What used to be my 6.2s on the Richter scale fell to mere tremors. Lilly was right. Things like programming problems, publicity debacles, script failures—these were common occurrences in my day. Not life or death, by any means.

Such a perspective was liberating. I became more efficient. I made day-to-day decisions without double-thinking myself. Things that might have threatened me before, like a star walkout, for example, no longer sent me into a tailspin. Erik

Estrada, the star of *CHiPs,* and Gary Coleman of *Diff'rent Strokes* both staged job actions during that year, as did Barbara Mandrell. She told me she was exhausted. She wanted to quit her variety show in midseason. But I had, by then, ultimately realized the power of saying no. And I said it, in effect, to all three. Barbara Mandrell did leave, but Estrada and Coleman returned to their respective series with a minimum of fuss when they understood I was not about to cave in.

If I sound confident about the idea of making an illness work in your favor, that may be because I'd had Hodgkin's disease once before. That was in 1974, when I was twenty-five and working at WLS in Chicago. I was diagnosed during a routine checkup, and because the disease was caught in stage one (the least serious stage), it was never considered life-threatening. The cure, however, felt much worse than the illness. I went through six months of radiation treatment, followed by twelve weeks of relatively mild "prophylactic chemotherapy." My hair didn't fall out, but my weight dropped from 170 to 135, and the rough humor around the office—where only a few people knew what was wrong with me—went, "You must play poker, Brandon, because you look like you lost your ass in a card game." I vomited frequently and felt sluggish all the time, but I never missed a day's work.

This time, though, the situation was different, for several reasons. Instead of being an anonymous assistant promo man at a local station, I was the head of programming at a network. I had to appear at press conferences, affiliate meetings, and industry gatherings. Instead of being single, I was married and now had a child. And instead of being in stage one,

I was being treated, because I'd recurred, as if I were in stage four. Not to be overly dramatic, but this *was* a matter of life and death.

It was an old college friend who first suggested that something was seriously wrong with me. Ira Bergman was a pediatric neurologist in Pittsburgh. While passing through L.A. one day, he looked me up, and we went running together. During the run, I began to cough, and the coughing brought on some questions from Ira. I told him that I wasn't crazy about my doctor, a cancer specialist who at times seemed more interested in selling me a script his kid had written on spec for *Hill Street Blues* than in listening to what I was telling him about the swollen glands in my neck.

As soon as I mentioned that I'd had five biopsies in the last two years, Ira's tone changed. "I don't want to alarm you," he said. "But I think you ought to get another doctor immediately. I think there's something wrong with you, and by the time this guy figures out what it is, it could be too late." He gave me the name of Denny Slamon, a young oncological researcher who occasionally took on special cases. "He's the best," Ira said.

Slamon didn't just give me the standard tests; he rebiopsied every tissue sample that had ever been taken from me. He said he could detect Hodgkin's on a microscope slide that dated back to 1972, when I was diagnosed as having "cat scratch fever" in New Haven. And he told me I had Hodgkin's again. Or maybe I had Hodgkin's *still*. "God knows how long this has been in your system," he said. "I'm going to be as aggressive with the treatment as I can be. I'm going to give it to you with both barrels. Last time was a tea party compared to what you're going to get now."

I actually got two different kinds of treatment in alternating sessions. The first was called MOPP, then the standard cocktail for treating Hodgkin's. The other was called ABVD. At the time ABVD was still experimental in the United States, but had been used with great success in Italy. Eight different chemicals would be delivered into my vein each month. I would react, Slamon told me, like a boxer who is game but overmatched. In other words, the first time I got "knocked down" by the treatment, I would get off the canvas feeling relatively fresh and resilient. But over time I would get worn out physically and mentally until I was surviving strictly on will. The chemicals would make me bloated, change the shape of my face, and make my hair fall out. I would have no feeling in my fingers and my feet. I would have mood swings, and my appetite would be unpredictable. Furthermore, after nine heavyweight rounds of this, the UCLA staff would harvest my bone marrow for use in the event that I contracted leukemia from the treatment. That procedure alone would have a devastating effect on my body.

I went for my monthly treatments at the Factor Building at UCLA, usually on Friday afternoons, so I'd have my worst days over the weekend and miss a minimum amount of work. First, I would get a pill for nausea, then, a half hour later, a sleeping pill. After that, I would sit down in a hard plastic office chair, and the chemotherapy would start. After about an hour, it was over. The usual postchemo routine was that I'd get driven home by Lilly, and then I'd throw up and pass out. Always, I wore the same sweater, a misshapen maroon-colored cardigan that had once been given to me as a Christmas present by Lorne Michaels's manager, Bernie Brillstein. "God, I'm sick of looking at that thing," Denny once said to me. "Why don't you get rid of it?"

"Are you kidding?" I said. "This is the perfect sweater to puke on."

Sometimes there were complications. As I got deeper into the treatment schedule, my veins atrophied and became harder to tap. If the IV slipped, the poison that was meant to kill the cancer would go into a muscle instead of my vein. I'd have an immediate reaction—a hideous swelling and acute pain. An alarm on the IV would go off, and people would come running. I've blocked a lot out from this period, but I do have a sketchy memory of someone frantically applying ice packs to my bicep area, and a nurse crying.

Ten days after each treatment, you reach what is called your nadir. That's when your white-blood-cell count is at its lowest, and you are most prone to pneumonia and other infections. You are supposed to take it easy during this time and stay out of crowds. I behaved myself after my first treatment at UCLA, and my nadir came and went without incident. But after my second treatment—exactly ten days after my second treatment—I served as best man at my friend Scott Siegler's wedding. There were about a hundred people there, and since Scott worked at a television studio and his wife, Dorothy, was an actress, many of the guests were in show business. What this meant was that I stayed around longer than I should have, chatting with people like Albert Brooks,

Christine Lahti, and Kathleen Turner. By the time Lilly and I got home, I was running a fever; the next morning my temperature was 103. I called Denny, told him what I'd done, and his response was swift: "You're in the hospital, pal." Sitting in the waiting room, I began to yell at myself for being so stupid—an excellent way, let me tell you, to turn a few heads. I had wanted to be the perfect patient, so the therapy would have every possible chance of success. I couldn't believe how I'd screwed up so early in the game.

At least one aspect of my treatment was proceeding right on schedule—the side effects of chemotherapy. The mood elevator in my chemical cocktail made me manic. I'd see decent ratings for the premiere of a show like *Mama's Family*, and I'd be so happy that I'd want to open my windows à la *Network* and yell the news. Bad news would spiral me into a grand funk that I think alarmed even Denny Slamon. And of course my hair fell out. I was prepared for that. As soon as I started chemo, I went to be fitted for a wig at the Celebrity House of Hair. On the way out, I passed Jimmy Stewart, who was coming in. Although we knew each other, we both averted our eyes.

One day deep into my dangerous year, I was watching Mr. T shoot thirty-second promos for *The A-Team* on the NBC lot. The show hadn't even been on the air yet, but everything about it was looking terrific. "T," I said excitedly, "get ready, because the next year is going to be something incredible—the best year of your life." He just sat there quietly for a moment, fingering the gold chains that hung around his neck. Then he said, "Yeah, I just hope it don't fuck with my head." Mr. T is one very deep dude—but I couldn't leave it at that. I had to flag down a passing NBC photographer and get him to fire off some shots to commemorate the moment. "Look," I said. "The two Mr. T's. This is gonna be great."

I got the prints back the next day, and what I saw was horrifying. There was the real Mr. T standing next to someone with a sickly complexion and an oddly bloated face, topped off with a close-out item from the Hair Club for Men: me. "Oh my God," I thought, "who am I kidding? *This* is what people are really seeing when they look at me." I threw away the prints, then called the photographer and told him to destroy the negatives.

I was saying, a while back, that cancer keeps you focused on what's important.

What was *supremely* important to me, at that affiliate reps meeting in Palm Springs, was that I not cede one inch of my turf. To do so would have been to admit that the disease was beating me. But beyond that, I had worked hard for the last two seasons to turn things around at NBC, and though the ratings didn't reflect it yet, I was sure that good things were about to happen. Quality shows like *Cheers, Hill Street Blues, Family Ties, St. Elsewhere,* and *Remington Steele,* the class shows of '82 that were slowly but surely building big followings. *The A-Team* was waiting in the wings. When those shows started to have an impact, dramatic changes were going to occur in terms of NBC's standing in the industry. I wanted to be there when those changes happened.

Grant Tinker's support was not just appreciated, it was necessary. In an industry plagued by the quick fix, Grant stood out as a paragon of patience. Still, the idea that the affiliates were lobbying to take my position away from me filled me with rage. I think Ray Timothy could see that as we faced each other in the La Quinta lobby.

"Ray," I said, "you should know that if you guys ever want to take away any piece of what I have, you might as well take it all, because I'm not going to be around to do two thirds or three quarters of what I'm doing now. I should be getting more responsibility, not less."

Ray just looked at me for a minute. Then he smiled and said, "By the way, that was the biggest goddamn Mexican I've ever seen."

August 5, 1983, and I am in a very different place—professionally, emotionally, and physically—from where I was exactly a year ago. This is the day my chemo ends, and so does a very long and dismal era at NBC. We are threatening to vacate the ratings cellar and, though we don't know it yet, headed for the kind of success unparalleled in network television. Our newer shows are not only winning critical raves, they're starting to get the kind of viewership that attracts attention: from sponsors, from the more sought-after producers, writers, and actors in the business—even, believe it or not, from the affiliates.

About a week later, I am in a meeting when someone on my staff comes in and says, "I'm sorry to interrupt, Brandon, but it's just been announced that NBC got one hundred thirty-three Emmy nominations. That's the most we've ever gotten, and it's more nominations than the other two networks combined."

I excuse myself from the meeting, walk down the hall, and lock myself in the bathroom. And there, poring over the pages of the Emmy tally sheets—the culmination of one hell of a year—I finally break down and cry.

FOUR

....

The Tartikoff
Channel

Y
ou're lucky if, as a program-
mer, you get a show crafted for your network that you yourself
would be canceling dinner plans in order not to miss. And
you're really lucky if somebody asks you to write a book about
shows like that. Then you get to fantasize in print about a
whole prime-time schedule composed of any shows in history,
shows that would keep you in front of the tube every night for
twenty-two hours a week.

I've tried to put my dream week together so that in each
night all the shows would fit together well and flow perfectly,
one to the next. The following program schedule is just that:
my favorites.

THE TARTIKOFF CHANNEL

	MONDAY	TUESDAY	WEDNESDA
7:00			
7:30			
8:00	LAUGH-IN	THE BEVERLY HILLBILLIES	BONANZA
8:30		THE ANDY GRIFFITH SHOW	
9:00	THE MARY TYLER MOORE SHOW	THE DICK VAN DYKE SHOW	THE FUGITIVE
9:30	MURPHY BROWN	SOAP	
10:00	THE SMOTHERS BROTHERS COMEDY HR.	FAMILY	ST. ELSEWHERE
10:30			

I think I'm like a lot of people on Monday nights. I come home and realize I've got four more days of work to trudge through. That's why I'd like to laugh on this night. Monday has historically been a great night for comedy for this reason. I've book-ended the night with the hip, topical, comedy-variety of *Laugh-In* and *The Smothers Brothers* and packed the middle with the two great ensemble comedies from the same gene pool, *Mary Tyler Moore* and *Murphy Brown*.

Even though I'm from the Northeast, two of my favorite shows growing up were "rural" comedies: *The Beverly Hillbillies* and *The Andy Griffith Show*. Their folksy characters are appealing to this day. *The Dick Van Dyke Show* from the same era made "easygoing" work in a show-biz setting. Susan Harris's *Soap* was the most inventive comedy of the seventies for me. And *Family* was the first show I got to supervise when I got to NBC. Plus it had great, thought-provoking drama in the comfort of a family setting.

Drama seems to be forgotten form these days. I yearn for a ni that would have stor lines as diverse as th ones I've scheduled here. Yet what qualit I wanted to be Little in *Bonanza*. I wante to catch the one-arm guy in *The Fugitive*, and I wanted my sta to never tell me abou plots in developmen for *St. Elsewhere*, s could watch it at hor just like you.

THURSDAY	FRIDAY	SATURDAY	SUNDAY
			60 MINUTES
COSBY SHOW	THE SIMPSONS	ALL IN THE FAMILY	THE ED SULLIVAN SHOW
HER KNOWS BEST	GET SMART	SANFORD AND SON	
ERS	THE TWILIGHT ZONE	THE GOLDEN GIRLS	PERRY MASON
FALO BILL	ALFRED HITCHCOCK PRESENTS	THE GEORGE BURNS AND GRACIE ALLEN SHOW	
STREET BLUES	THE ROCKFORD FILES	MISSION IMPOSSIBLE	THE UNTOUCHABLES

THURSDAY	FRIDAY	SATURDAY	SUNDAY
l, as Gomer Pyle uld say, "Surprise! prise! Surprise!" All one of these series e put on our "best t of television on vision" Thursday up of the eighties. hammocked my orite family show n my childhood, *her Knows Best*, ween *Cosby* and *ers*. If you're prised by *Buffalo* (since I was the who canceled it), mit the cancellation s a crime. But hey, statute of limitations p. If you're going to st me anyway, ugh, do it on *Hill* *et*, the best cop w ever.	The reality is, no one wants reality at the start of a weekend. The opening comedy bloc of *The Simpsons* and *Get Smart* are shows I could watch with my daughter and each of us could laugh for different reasons. I lived for *The Twilight Zone* on Friday nights, and I tried to revive the Hitchcock anthology at NBC in 1985. I don't care much about detective shows, but since Jim Rockford didn't care much about being a detective, his worked for me (and NBC on Friday nights).	With these classic comedy shows, I'd never feel deprived staying home on Saturday night. From Archie to *Sanford* to *The Golden Girls*, the characters are richly drawn and the comedy edgy and loud—just the way I like it. I love George Burns and how he broke "the fourth wall" to talk to us directly about Gracie. *Mission Impossible* is the ultimate escape show where the skill of the writers equaled the skill of the team on screen.	It's hard to get families to watch television together these days. Too many sets in the house, too many channels to choose from. But I'm a traditionalist at heart, and the programming this night—*60 Minutes*, *Ed Sullivan*, *Perry Mason*, and *The Untouchables*—would revive that kind of viewing. It would be an awesome night in the ratings!

FIVE

....

Wanted: Thirty-Five-
Year-Old Leading Men
and Beautiful Women
Who Are Funny

S uppose I describe a TV show for you. It's about three people who work together in an office: two men and a woman. One of the men is older; his children are probably out of college by now; he's settled into life, enjoying himself. The other man and the woman are younger, attractive, kind of Yuppie-ish—but not romantically involved. They can talk to each other as friends, and this helps them cope with the challenges of the office and the larger world beyond.

If this sounds familiar, that's not surprising.

The show is already on the air.

It's called the *Today* show.

All of television comes down to casting. And I'm not just talking about sitcoms, police dramas, and TV movies. The same rule applies to news, sports, and even game shows: If you like the faces and personalities who are on the screen, you'll want to stay tuned. If you don't, then nothing else about the program makes much difference—it's only a matter of time before you'll be changing channels.

The story of Oprah Winfrey, for example, involves no great creative leaps or broadcasting innovations. It's a triumph of casting, pure and simple. Phil Donahue was already on the scene, playing the part of Sensitive, Understanding Man, the kind of guy women could confide in when their husbands were not around. Sally Jessy Raphaël came along later to represent the Somewhat Older Woman Who Goes Back to Work After Spending Years Raising Her Family. But Oprah was always the Typical Viewer. Intelligent, but not so smart that she didn't have to ask a lot of commonsense questions. Attractive, but not some kind of perfect show-biz specimen who didn't have to watch what she wore and struggle with her weight. Her show consisted of the basic bleachers and a microphone—the cheapest kind of show in television. Her local Chicago production was essentially no different from the kind of television that was produced in the fifties. It made it to the big time based on nothing but her talent and the character she "portrayed," i.e., herself.

It follows then that actors and other TV personalities are the key players in the medium—the means by which viewers connect to a show. The people on the screen serve the audience as surrogate friends, parents, and lovers. Without them a TV executive is nothing. But finding good performers, and then "managing" them for the successful run of a show, is tougher than you might think.

Let's clear up one myth right away—the myth that there are about two dozen fantastic actors out there for every available role. If only that were the case. It *is* true that in New York and L.A. every waiter, bartender, and aerobics instructor is really an aspiring actor. And yes, huge crowds often do turn out for a casting call. But that doesn't change the fact that, in trying to put together a network show, you often find yourself (a) settling for someone who doesn't quite fit the part or (b) coming up empty. Sometimes in a casting session you can get the same feeling as when you ponder the current crop of political candidates: "In a nation of 250 million people, is this *really* the best we can do?"

Of course there are times when you put out a traditional casting call and you do wind up with an embarrassment of riches. When we were casting for *The Cosby Show* and *The Golden Girls,* for example, each part was so deep in qualified people that we could have put together five national road companies of the show. The cast for *The Golden Girls*—Bea Arthur, Rue McClanahan, Estelle Getty, and Betty White—was like an all-star team of comic actresses. Each of those women could have fronted her own show—and three had. The show without them would have been just as well written, but not half as good or as valuable. Still, none of that is surprising, just a matter of supply and demand. Blame it on Hollywood—or the society that Hollywood mirrors and serves—but there simply aren't that many worthy parts written for women, as the French say, "of a certain age," or, in the case of *Cosby*, black actors. Venture into those areas, and you're fishing in a pond stocked with talent.

When you're casting the key roles for most shows, though, you're not talking ponds; you're talking puddles.

One of the hardest "types" to find, year in and year out, is the Beautiful Woman Who Is Also Funny. Lucille Ball in the 1950s was probably the classic example of this rarest of species, and then of course there's Mary Tyler Moore. Bill Persky, the Emmy Award–winning writer-director of *The Dick Van Dyke Show* and *Kate & Allie*, has a theory about why attractiveness and wit are so seldom found in the same actress. "We live in a chauvinistic world," he once said to me, "and if a woman is good-looking, she learns very early on that that goes a long way in society, and she really doesn't have to be anything else. It's the women who *can't* get by on their looks," he said, "who are forced to develop a sense of humor as a way of compensating and competing." Chauvinism in casting is a fact of life in America and, unfortunately, still a larger fact of life in Hollywood. Slowly but surely, though, the walls are tumbling down. The "casting" of Katie Couric on the *Today* show is an example of this. And, of course, Candice Bergen, Julia Louis-Dreyfus, Kirstie Alley, Jasmine Guy, and Susan Dey are all bringing to life role models for contemporary American women.

Thirty-five-year-old leading men, however, are still the ultimate Holy Grails of Hollywood. If an actor is handsome, is skilled at his craft, and has a good track record, he has probably moved on. Today's movies are filled with those "bankable" graduates. Stars like Bruce Willis, Michael Keaton, Tom

Hanks, Michael J. Fox, Billy Crystal, Chevy Chase, Bill Murray, Steve Martin, and Eddie Murphy are all émigrés from the small screen. As a result, when you make a casting call for leading men, what you often see are actors from one of two categories: the Pretty Boys who look great in the *Vanity Fair* ads but often can't act their way out of their Guess jeans, and a second group that I call the Usual Suspects. The latter are the guys who seem to do nothing but travel from audition to audition, their résumés littered with busted pilots or series that lasted about eight episodes.

The sight of the Usual Suspects sitting in the anteroom of a casting office is enough to make a network executive's heart sink, assuming he has one. This is why the day we cast Don Johnson in *Miami Vice* was one of the most frustrating days of my NBC career.

A little background is probably in order. *Miami Vice* had its genesis in a vague idea I had about getting an MTV sensibility into a cop show. I say "idea," but to paraphrase Woody Allen in *Annie Hall,* it was more of a springboard on the way to a concept that could be fleshed out into an idea. So the operative word in this story is not so much "idea," but MTV.

I was obsessed with it.

When *Time* magazine trumpeted Bob Pittman's phenomenon on its cover, I spent every watching moment of the next week at home, gorging myself on the smorgasbord of nonstop visual imagery MTV provided. I suspected Lilly was off in the next room dialing the Betty Ford Center to see if they took people suffering from "video overdose."

There have been a lot of apocryphal stories written about how the words "MTV Cops" were scribbled on a napkin, and

presto—out popped *Miami Vice*. What hasn't been written is
that the first dozen or so producers who were shown that
napkin thought that Jeff Sagansky and I were totally fried—
that the job had finally taken too many of our brain cells
prisoner.

Enter Tony Yerkovich, the Emmy Award–winning writer
(*Hill Street Blues*). When we gave him the pitch in stereo, he
got it immediately. He combined it with a flashy idea *he* had
about Florida, and came up with one of the best pilot scripts
we'd ever read. It had great texture, great dialogue, great
characters. The original working title was "Gold Coast," and
agents who'd read it were calling to say, "Congratulations—
you've got the best pilot script of the season. Knock 'em
dead." So I was confounded when the best we could do for
the Sonny Crockett part was *Don Johnson.*

What you have to understand is that when this was happening in 1984, Don Johnson did not exactly have a great track
record in the TV business. He had been in about six pilots,
all of which had failed. He had been beaten out by David
Hasselhoff, a soap-opera actor, for the lead in *Knight Rider,*
a show in which a *car* was the real star. Don was classically
handsome. Just about every man in America would love to
walk around in his skin for a week. And he had developed into
a pretty good actor, which is why he'd gotten up to the plate
six times before. But he did seem that afternoon like the
ultimate Usual Suspect.

So why did we even consider him? Because of the severe
shortage of thirty-five-year-old leading men—and because we
were in such a rush to get the pilot shot. The competition for
Sonny Crockett, in fact, came down to just two people. One

was Larry Wilcox, best know as the white-bread guy who rode the motorcycle next to Erik Estrada on *CHiPs*. Don was the other.

"You know, Don's good, but he's been around. We've got a great script. Are you sure he's the best we can come up with?" I asked Michael Mann, the executive producer.

But Mann told me not to look at it that way. "Think of Tom Selleck," he said. "Selleck failed in *seven* pilots. And then somebody put him on *Magnum, P.I.* and now he's the biggest star on television."

So I went along. Not that I had much choice.

Then Mann and Yerkovich delivered the pilot. The dialogue crackled, the characters were fresh, inventive. Philip Michael Thomas was superb as the cop from New York who had come to Miami to find his brother's killer. Each of the subsidiary characters was unique, particularly Edward James Olmos, who brought a brilliant inscrutability to the role of Lieutenant Castillo. He gave tension and mystery to a part that would have been predictable in any other cop series.

There was *nothing* predictable about this pilot. It was all pastels and hip clothing and rock music and totally, totally contemporary. One sequence especially made the hair stand up on the back of my neck, made me feel that the show had hit some kind of sweet spot. Sonny Crockett was driving his car down an open highway. It was a hot night, the wind was blowing through his hair, and a Phil Collins number was playing in the background. The scene looked like something out of the movie *Breathless*.

More important, it looked like nothing I'd ever seen on TV. I knew right then that *Miami Vice* would transform television.

It would make all other cop shows look like leisure suits. But just as big a transformation had taken place within Don Johnson himself. He had somehow made a giant leap of self-confidence. This wasn't the same guy who'd been in NBC's pallid remake of *From Here to Eternity*. His performance reminded me of those old movies where the football coach pulls a player off the bench and says, "You're our quarterback now: Go out there and show those guys what you can do!"—and magic happens. Johnson had nailed the part. He was on top of his game as an actor. It was a beautiful thing to see. Somehow, too, age had transformed his pretty-boy looks into a rugged, smart, sexy, yet approachable television presence.

At this moment, the chemistry was perfect. We had a major hit in the making. And a major star.

It can get pretty tense at a casting session. A lot is at stake for the actors. If they get the part that they're auditioning for and the show is a hit, they'll become famous. And that changes everything. An actor or actress who's been on unemployment or living on welfare can suddenly find themselves a year later living in a house in Malibu, with two cars in the driveway and a lot of money in the bank. But it isn't just the actors who contribute to the pressure-packed atmosphere. The producers, directors, and executives on hand are also extremely edgy because the decisions they're about to make could have a profound effect on *their* lives and careers.

How uncomfortable does it get in those sterile-looking, ten-by-fifteen-foot casting rooms?

Well, let's put it this way: Fred De Cordova, the venerable

producer of *The Tonight Show* with Johnny Carson, once re-marked that it would be wonderful if all entertainment executives came equipped with a built-in dissolve switch, one that they could use to escape from unpleasant situations. "You'd just turn on this thing," Fred said, "dissolve yourself out, and *poof!* you'd be into the next scene." I can think of more than a few casting sessions when I would have been tempted to reach for that switch. Yet I went out of my way to be at as many as possible. Why? Because you can spend a year refining the concept of a show and working on the script, and if the wrong person gets cast in a crucial role, the party is over. The idea and the words are vital, but without the right talent to realize them, you're finished.

What was I looking for at those sessions? Originals. Special beings who were different from the performers already on television. Personalities that you could picture being on the cover of *People* magazine within a year. Actors and actresses who were chameleons, who could make themselves and the scripts into something you'd never seen or heard before. What makes the casting process endurable and, at times, even fascinating is that you always hope that the magic might be just around the corner.

Once, when I was watching a rough cut of the third episode of *Miami Vice,* an actor in one of the supporting parts seemed to suddenly pop off the screen. He was playing a truly unappealing character, a small-time hood who beat his wife. And he was hardly what you'd call traditionally telegenic. His face, while rugged, seemed a bit jowly, and his hairline receded into a widow's peak. But his performance was so commanding that his quirky looks somehow became part of the whole package. He was one of those actors who simply had great presence. Star presence.

I immediately called producer Stephen Cannell, who was developing a detective show for NBC that would eventually be called *Stingray*.

"I've just found a guy I think is perfect for the lead. Take a look at this tape I'm sending over and tell me what you think," I said. "Casting told me his name is Bruce Willis."

The next day, Cannell called me back excitedly. "He's great," he said. "I'm going to send him our script right now. But by the way, we've already checked on him. We'd be in second position to ABC. He's up for a series there, and they've already called him back several times. Lew Erlicht is worried he's not really a leading man type. He's hoping to get a 'name' into the part, and if they do we'll have a clean shot at him."

As soon as Cannell laid out that scenario my heart sank. I put two and two together, and realized how I, in a recent attempt to screw someone, had probably screwed myself. That very week Robert Blake had stormed into my office and pitched me the idea for his *Hell Town* movie-of-the-week. That much I've told you already. What I didn't say then, though, was that one of the reasons I said yes to Blake's project was that he'd baited me. That is, he told me he had a standing offer to do a detective series at ABC and I had to act immediately. So, I thought to myself, I can get his movie and I can diminish the ABC series at the same time by depriving them of the star power they're looking for.

What happened? When I took Blake out of play, I'd forced ABC to cast about for a new face. Bruce Willis. Willis got the job and he went on to help make that ABC series—*Moonlight-ing*—a megahit.

Almost as important as listening to actors read is just watching them walk in and out of the room. How do they carry themselves? Are they nervous? When you throw a question at them, ostensibly to break the ice, do they have a natural humor about them? How are they dressed? How much enthusiasm do they show?

People ask me if aspiring actresses ever come on to me, hoping that will help them get a part. I tell them that the closest I ever came to something like that was when we were auditioning women for a part in a pilot about a sort of female James Bond. The lead needed to be both a martial-arts expert and a seductress. One by one the actresses came in and tried to show their great range. My eyes were beginning to glaze over when another actress came in, read a few lines, then put down the script and began unzipping her skintight leather pants. She had a bodysuit on underneath, but still, I was shocked. Then suddenly one of her spike heels got caught on the hem of her pants leg. She hopped up and down, spun around, said, "Oh, shit," and staggered toward the door. I'll never forget the sight of her leaving the audition room with her torn pants over one arm—without the part.

Stripping may not win points at an audition, but wanting the job does. You do get an A for effort. Making a TV show is hard work, and if an actor doesn't seem to want the role badly enough at the outset, the arrangement rarely works.

Fred Gwynne, from *The Munsters* and *Car 54, Where Are You?*, was one of my all-time favorite character actors. He once expressed interest in a certain new series that NBC was then planning to put on the air. His eagerness surprised us, since we had been offering him roles for years and he had always said no. He was what's known in the business as a "tough get." Now, a rather simple little sitcom about an orphan, *Punky Brewster,* had attracted his attention. Since the role that was at stake was as the little girl's guardian, I wondered what was up. As it turned out, Gwynne had always been interested in children's entertainment and what kids were seeing on the tube. He'd taken to writing children's books himself and wanted to make sure that the children of America were getting good, positive messages.

On the day he was to read for the part, Fred was dressed elegantly—almost entirely in white. With his black hair slicked back, he had an entirely new look. I was struck by this. His new image was no accident. He clearly wanted to repackage himself.

Then came the moment for little Soleil Moon Frye, the six-and-a-half-year-old girl who'd already been cast as Punky Brewster, to meet the man she'd be reading with. The door flew open, and she bounded onto the couch where Fred Gwynne was sitting. "Hello, young lady," Fred said to her.

"Hi," she said right back. Then, without missing a beat, she added, "Hey, aren't you Herman Munster?"

So much for "An actor prepares." Fred couldn't conceal his dismay at seeing his elaborate transformation undone by a little girl. He ended up giving what was far from his best reading. As much as he had wanted it, the part eventually went to George Gaynes.

The hardest-working actor I ever saw at an audition was George Peppard reading for the part of Colonel John "Hannibal" Smith, the leader of the *A-Team*. Peppard, at that point, was at a kind of career crossroads. His last acting job had been in the pilot of *Dynasty*, but he had been so demanding on the production that he'd been replaced. Peppard, by Hollywood standards, was damaged goods coming into the *A-Team* audition, and on some level he knew it. Outwardly, though, he looked as cool and cocky as the character he was playing, but his blue shirt kept getting darker and darker as he read his lines. Remember the movie *Broadcast News?* Remember Albert Brooks sweating through his debut as an anchorman? That's what I'm talking about here. As I watched Peppard audition I was thinking, Here's a guy who's done thousands of hours of television and film but he's still nervous. Maybe Peppard was afraid that *The A-Team* might be his last shot at anything worthwhile. Whatever the case, he was out there trying—and succeeding.

There are times, of course, when an actor can get a little too intense for his own good. I am thinking of the time William Devane auditioned for the lead role in *Cheers*. We were extremely excited about the show's prospects right from the start. For one thing, Shelley Long, one of the beautiful *and* funny people, was the front-runner as Diane. Producers Glen and Les Charles had delivered a funny and literate script, and we had one of the great comedy directors in television with Jim Burrows. But who were we kidding? Without an actor for the pivotal role of Sam Malone, we only had a show that looked good on paper.

One of the finalists for the part was Fred Dryer, the ex-pro-football player who would eventually become a star on *Hunter*. Dryer *was* Sam in many ways, but there was some concern, at that point in his career, about his inexperience as an actor.

Bachelor number two was Ted Danson. He was the middle-of-the-road candidate. One vocal high-ranking NBC executive thought he was all wrong—too much of a character actor (an impression based on his performance in *Body Heat*) and not enough of a leading man.

William Devane had to be considered the leading candidate for the role. He had the most impressive credits, and had the most experience as a leading man. But somehow he'd forgotten that Golden Rule of show business: Unless you're up for the part of Tarzan, never audition in bare feet. Devane, either because he was feeling a bit cocky or because of his training, felt that he just *had* to perform Sam's part with no shoes or socks on; he saw the character as some macho guy who would go around in just slacks and a T-shirt. The problem was that in doing the first scene, where Sam is supposed to be cleaning up behind the *Cheers* bar, Devane accidentally dropped a glass. He could have stopped, waited for the broken glass to be swept up and tried the scene again. But that would have been wimping out—and wimping out in front of the network honchos to boot. So instead, he pressed on, even though there were big shards of glass all around his feet. He was trying hard not to wreck the mood he'd so carefully created on Stage 25 at Paramount that afternoon. But he was clearly distracted and began screwing up his usually impeccable timing. The Charles brothers and Burrows had been leaning toward Devane, but this performance caused them to cast their lot with Danson. NBC agreed, and eleven years later, he still has his Emmy Award–winning part. He's become one of the best-known faces in America and a millionaire many times over. And even the dissenting NBC executive, if you could find him, would probably admit that Ted turned out to be a pretty good leading man.

I could get pretty intense about my search for The Next Great Face. Just ask David Hasselhoff, who has told people that the first time he saw me, he thought I was gay. Well, I *was* openly staring at him on that flight from Las Vegas to L.A., but it had nothing to do with romance.

Hasselhoff and I were both coming back from the National Association of Television Programming Executives convention. Earlier that day, at the hotel where I was staying, I had witnessed grown women leaving their slot machines to walk clear across the casino to get Hasselhoff's autograph. For any of you who have been to Vegas, that's a pretty powerful barometer of personal magnetism. I knew he was an actor on *The Young and the Restless,* and when I spotted him sitting several rows behind me on the plane, I started to plan my approach.

Ordinarily, I would have just introduced myself to Hasselhoff, but because of turbulence, the seat-belt sign remained on during the flight. All I could do was twist around in my seat every few minutes and look back at him. "This guy would be perfect for *Knight Rider,*" I said to Larry Lyttle, a close friend and prominent TV studio executive who was sitting beside me. "I could make him a big star."

"Jesus, Tartikoff," Larry said, "don't you ever turn off the meter?"

Knight Rider was conceived to compensate for the scarcity

of leading men on television. "I want to do *The Lone Ranger* with a car," producer Glen Larson had proclaimed in his pitch. "Kind of a sci-fi thing with the soul of a Western." The idea was that the show's main character spoke only about six words per episode. Our Western-type hero wouldn't be saddled with a lot of dialogue. The only range he'd need was an open stretch of land to drive by in his car.

We eventually signed Hasselhoff for the show, and he looked fine driving around in his incredibly high-tech, talking (hey, *somebody* had to talk) Pontiac Trans-Am. The ratings were good and Hasselhoff was happy—until one Friday afternoon in the third season, when he walked off the set and said he wasn't coming back until he got a substantial raise. Our response to his agent was also six words: "Tell him the car's the star."

As you know, Hasselhoff walked *back* that Monday.

Knight Rider wasn't TV drama at its best, by any means, but it was one of the few shows I can think of that was casting-proof.

I always felt that the three best clubs in my bag were casting, casting, and casting, but in truth a lot comes down to serendipity. Gary Nardino, who was president of Paramount Television, once asked me if I'd like to fly to Vegas with him to see the Larry Holmes–Gerry Cooney fight. I'd never been to a boxing match before—or since—but this sounded like fun. We'd have a private plane, ringside seats—I said, "Sure." What impressed me most, though, was the VIP party we went to beforehand. Many of Hollywood's notables were there, causing their usual stir. But the person getting the most attention—the one Sylvester Stallone and Ryan O'Neal were gushing over—was a guy sitting off in the corner who I'd never heard of before. A guy named Mr. T.

Mr. T was dressed that night in a black T-shirt and sweat pants. He had his trademark Mohawk haircut and about forty pounds of gold jewelry on his fingers and around his neck. Mr. T was a professional bodyguard whose primary experience in show business consisted of a brief appearance in *Rocky III.* But when the people at the party gawked at him or asked for his autograph, T was perfectly at ease with the attention, and acted like a man who'd been born to the spotlight. At that point, the idea for *The A-Team* was still percolating in my mind—and in the mind of Steve Cannell, who had been pitched the bare bones of a TV show that was supposed to combine the style of *The Dirty Dozen, The Magnificent Seven, Mission Impossible,* and *The Road Warrior.* I had a sense that Mr. T's outrageousness would somehow fit into that show—once, of course, someone figured out exactly what the show was.

As soon as I got back to L.A., NBC signed T for a guest appearance on *Silver Spoons.* Steve Cannell was invited to the taping. After that show he and NBC were convinced that we had our first member of The A-Team.

Mr. T is an example of real serendipity. But occasionally I've been in the exact right place at the exact right time and missed the get. Like when I passed on *Roseanne.*

Sad but true. Marcy Carsey and Tom Werner brought me the idea back when Roseanne Arnold's last name was Barr and her standup act was just starting to catch on. I had never seen her live, but I had looked at some tapes of her *Tonight*

Show appearances and an HBO special and concluded that she didn't have that necessary twinkle in her eye when she did her jokes about being an oppressed housewife. "I don't know, she doesn't seem to have a TV likability to me," I said to Tom and Marcy. "She looks like she's snarling at the audience." We did offer them a pilot, but when Brandon Stoddard, my counterpart over at ABC, guaranteed them twelve episodes, they jumped at the better deal.

Roseanne, of course, went on to become one of the biggest success stories of the last decade. And it's no mystery why: I was wrong, she does have *great* TV eyes. What I took for nastiness is just a devilish glint. A few years ago Lilly and I attended a dinner for the L.A. Free Clinic and found ourselves seated at the same table as Roseanne and Tom Arnold. Throughout the entire evening, she was constantly looking for a way to get into mischief. When she wasn't trying to shock Harvey Korman's wife she would say things to me like, "I'm gonna fire all the writers on my show. Maybe I would have been better off at your network instead of ABC."

If only that had been the case—I would have just had to go into work twice a week.

It's hard to find new stars, yes. But working with great old TV legends is not without its own perils, either. Once when NBC was so far back in last place that I thought we could lay claim to being the original fourth network, Fred Silverman was desperate to get *something* on the schedule that would at least get sampled, and he decided that the salvation of the network lay in signing television icons.

"Get me James Arness!" said Fred.

Now *that* got my attention. I'd grown up watching *Gunsmoke*, and to me Arness was more a legend from the Golden Age of TV than a real person. Hey, we're talking about *Marshal Matt Dillon* here. The first thing we did was to call Tom Tannenbaum over at MGM Television. They had just announced a deal with Eric Bercovici, who had done *Shōgun* for us. Eric was free and willing to develop a property for Arness at NBC. He spun a two-hour script called *McLain's Law* about a retired cop who put the blues back on to avenge the murder of his closest friend. Tannenbaum approved the project and wasted no time in kissing Arness into the package.

"Well," I said jubilantly to Fred, "I got Arness."

"You did? That's great. How's he looking these days?"

Pregnant pause. After all, we had a deal.

"Gee, Fred, I don't know," I said. "I didn't talk to Arness. Tannenbaum handled that."

"Well, *I'm* not signing off on a series commitment," Fred said. "No one's seen this guy in years. How do I know he doesn't look like Gabby Hayes, for chrissakes?"

I had no choice but to call Tannenbaum back and make up a story about how I needed to meet with Arness to discuss the creative direction of *McLain's Law*.

The unfortunate thing about bullshit, I've noticed over the years, is that it always sounds like bullshit.

Tannenbaum was a good sport about it, though. He and I drove out to the actor's relatively modest little house in Santa Monica. We walked up the pathway, rang the bell, and waited. I began praying that someone who still very much resembled Marshal Matt Dillon would be inside.

Suddenly the door flew open and I saw most—but not

all—of a massive body that was obviously over six and a half feet tall. Whose body it was, I couldn't tell for certain, because the head was someplace up above the doorframe.

For a long while nothing happened. Then Arness craned his neck down and stuck his famous and (thank goodness) well-preserved face through the doorway.

"Well, sonny," he growled, "how do I look?"

While *McLain's Law* failed to capture an audience in its one and only season on the air, it did indicate the route that Fred Silverman and NBC would travel successfully together in the eighties—the big difference, however, was that Fred was then a seller, not a buyer, of TV shows.

When he left the network in 1981, Fred jump-started an independent production company by creating a whole line of shows that slipped familiar, beloved actors into M.O.R. (middle-of-the-road) concepts. They were like comfortable shoes, as easy to live in as a pair of favorite broken-in loafers.

When I called Fred up and pitched him a show about a country *Columbo* with Andy Griffith as a courtroom lawyer, Fred didn't have to ask how Griffith "looked." He'd already seen a ten-minute clip from the NBC miniseries *Fatal Vision* that was about to air. The clip showed Andy playing a Southern-fried, seersuckered lawyer who cut his toenails on top of his office desk while talking to a client. *Matlock,* a distant cousin to that character, may not appeal to the youngest, hippest audience in America, but it's still pulling in solid audiences seven years later.

Fred soon peppered the airwaves with Carroll O'Connor in *In the Heat of the Night,* Raymond Burr in the new *Perry Mason,* and William Conrad in *Jake and the Fat Man.* And the shows succeeded in part because viewers were at ease inviting "old friends" into their living rooms. Television is an intimate medium, and the actors and actresses with whom we feel at ease have a natural advantage. A twenty-seven-inch television screen is tailor-made for close-ups the size of a real-life face, so we can look into their eyes and make a real human connection. When you stared into Carroll O'Connor's baby blues in *All in the Family,* you forgave Archie Bunker for all the awful (and hilarious) things that came out of his mouth.

To me, the biggest difference between movie stars and television stars is the "airport factor." If you saw a television star in an airport, would you hesitate to walk up and say hello? Probably not. Because you feel you know them. Even stars who portray despicable characters, like Ed O'Neill (*Married with Children*) or Larry Hagman (*Dallas*) are approachable. With movie stars, you'd be more inclined to keep a safe distance. After all, usually when you see movie stars you're in the dark and they're fifty feet high.

At crunch time—when we had to decide on crucial casting for series leads—I would always think of that "airport factor," especially knowing the next two factors would inevitably come into play: the "blurring syndrome" and "fame."

In most successful shows, the characters and the people playing them often "blur" together over time. The stars affect the same mannerisms, the same dress habits, the same ways of expressing themselves as their characters. Tom Selleck *is* Thomas Magnum. Corbin Bernsen has become *L.A. Law*'s Arnie Becker. Even *Cheers*'s Sam Malone seems to have mellowed over the past decade into a guy very reminiscent of

. . . Ted Danson. The producer's office of a successful show can have a revolving door, and the only continuity in a series may be the actors who go the distance. "Hey, I've been around here longer than anyone else. I know more than anyone else," they might say to themselves. "Maybe I should be the one who's in charge."

Frankly, this can sometimes be good news. Michael Landon's creative control of *Little House on the Prairie,* Fred Dryer's on *Hunter,* and Roseanne Arnold's on *Roseanne* made these shows sparkle. Then comes the bad news: More often than not the inevitable power plays begin. Fame, after all, is a very potent drug, and some can handle it better than others. The ones who can't, well . . . that's why you read so often about the stars who stage walkouts on their series. Of course, there's a lot of resentment when this happens—particularly from the audience.

Television, far more than movies, is a medium that creates its own stars. The networks may have afforded these performers the opportunity, but it's the audience that keeps them in the firmament. In the last few years, viewers can take the credit for launching the careers of Tim Allen (*Home Improvement*), Luke Perry and Jason Priestley (*Beverly Hills, 90210*), Janine Turner (*Northern Exposure*), Keenen Ivory Wayans and Damon Wayans (*In Living Color*), and two of my favorites, Will Smith (*Fresh Prince of Bel Air*) and Jerry Seinfeld (*Seinfeld*). On the other hand, if a star decides to walk out, the audience can suddenly turn on him.

If you've ever visited Hollywood, I'm sure you've seen street people selling "maps to the stars' homes." I've often fantasized about manufacturing "maps to the homes of stars who walked off." On my map you'd be able to locate where Pernell Roberts (*Bonanza*), McLean Stevenson (*M*A*S*H*), Suzanne Somers (*Three's Company*), and Shelley Long (*Cheers*) live now. I'd put stacks of these maps in the waiting rooms of every casting office and producer's suite.

Dealing with actors is complicated because you can never really know for sure when they're *acting*. They can dupe the most seasoned producer or network executive into believing anything.

One of the best performances I ever saw involved an actress who had a recurring role on *St. Elsewhere*. The producers of the show had created a story line in which she had a provocative encounter with a lesbian. So there the actress sat in Jeff Sagansky's office at NBC, bawling her eyes out, claiming the producers had inserted this scene because they knew about her own strict moral beliefs and were trying to induce her to quit the show. She was certain, she told us, they had her replacement waiting in makeup. By the end of the session, Jeff and I were welling up as well. "Why don't you guys just leave the poor girl alone?" Jeff later pleaded with Bruce Paltrow, the producer. "You're pushing her to the brink of a breakdown." Bruce laughed at us. "Congratulations, guys," he said. "She doesn't have the best range of any actress I've ever worked with, but the one trick in her bag is that she can cry on cue. And you bozos bought it!"

Dabney Coleman is one guy who really caught me off-balance. For two seasons, Coleman starred in a show on NBC called *Buffalo Bill,* in which he played an obnoxious, vituperative talk-show host. At the end of the first year, the show was doing only marginally well in the ratings, and we had a creative meeting to discuss some changes they might make to motivate us to go beyond the first thirteen episodes.

Coleman came in character as Buffalo Bill Bittinger, and he stayed that way for the entire hour and a half of the meeting. I'd never seen anything like it. When we ended on an inconclusive note, Coleman suddenly jumped up and leaned over right in my face. "So what are you saying to me, Brandon?" he was yelling. "*What are you saying?* Are you picking up the show for next season or not? Let me get this straight now—are you telling me that we're going to come back or that we're not? Because I'm getting all these nuances here." On one level he was kidding. But on another, his performance was very cagey. "Okay, Dabney," I finally said, "just knock it off. You're renewed. You're renewed." Whether Jay Tarses or Tom Patchett, his producers, had put Dabney up to this Bittinger-like performance, I don't know. All I did know was that Dabney was so great in the role that day, he deserved at least another season.

Speaking of producers, there was one (who shall remain nameless), a veteran of many cop shows, whose powers of deductive reasoning were called into play when a major star didn't just stage a performance—he vanished into thin air. The star (who shall also remain nameless) was demanding a large salary increase plus some pretty big perks. NBC and the studio balked at the demands and were getting ready to serve the star with papers when this disappearing act occurred. What to do?

"I can solve this," the producer said. With the skills he'd honed in his years of cop shows, he set his mind to work. First, where would the star hide? Easy. He'd want to lose himself in the biggest city in the world: New York. Second, where would he stay? In the hotel in that city where an episode of the series was recently shot. Third, would he be registered under his own name? No way. Stars always use an alias to protect themselves from civilians. And besides, this particular star had a favorite alias the producer knew about.

The producer placed a call to New York, got the hotel, asked to speak to the alias, and bingo! The star was subpoened in a matter of hours. The moral of the story: If you want to find an actor you have to get into character and think like that actor.

My showdown with Carroll O'Connor was a lot more straightforward. Carroll had precipitated it by throwing down the gauntlet to MGM Studios president David Gerber: Either he got control of *In the Heat of the Night* or he was not reporting back to the series. O'Connor had pulled this move in the seventies with what became known as *Archie Bunker's Place*— and he had won. When he tried it again with us, I was ten years into the job, and figured I could play poker with the best of them.

The scene: my office (any advantage helps). Warren Littlefield and I began by explaining to Carroll that the quality of his scripts would severely decline, because when word got out he was in charge, no topflight producer would sign on to the show. Then, of course, if he failed to appear on the set, there was the ugly possibility of a lawsuit.

I'll never forget how O'Connor looked at me then. He might have been smiling his Archie Bunker smile, but he responded with Chief Gillespie toughness:

"Well, you know, Brandon, I've been in California twenty

years," he said. "So when someone says to me, 'Did you know there was an earthquake this morning?' I say, 'Oh, really?' And that's exactly what I say when I hear the word 'lawsuit'— Oh, really?"

There was nothing else to do but try to call his bluff. I told Carroll we had explored whether Rod Steiger, who had originated the Gillespie role in the feature film, was available to step into the series. His representatives "hadn't said no."

That Hollywood double negative had dubious effect. Carroll replied matter-of-factly. "Rod Steiger is a consummate actor. I can find other things to do."

O'Connor had topped our hand and collected the pot. He took the reins of the series and the next year he won the Emmy for best actor in a television drama.

The one actor, however, who wins the unofficial award for exemplary behavior (and keeping his head on straight) during the successful run of a series is someone we didn't want to cast in the first place.

His name is Michael J. Fox.

We had absolutely no desire to give him the part of Alex Keaton in *Family Ties* after he read for us. We were bothered not by his comedy skills, which, as you know, are great, but by his height. How could someone that short have Michael Gross and Meredith Baxter Birney as his parents?

"It always annoyed me as a kid watching *Father Knows Best* that Bud Anderson was so much shorter than his parents," I said to Gary David Goldberg, the show's producer. "To me that undercut the credibility of the whole show. Let's not make that same mistake here."

Goldberg, however, was adamant about giving Fox the part. "This guy is amazing," he said. "You send him out to get two laughs, he comes back with five."

Goldberg is not a person who changes his mind easily, so I relented. "Go ahead if you insist," I said. "But I'm telling you, this is not the kind of face you'll ever see on a lunch box."

After the show had established itself as one of the biggest hits of the eighties and Michael J. Fox had starred in the box-office smash *Back to the Future,* he sent me a lunch box with his picture on it. I still have it in my office. Every once in a while, I open it up and read the note that Michael put inside. It says, "Eat crow, Tartikoff."

P.S.

I've often wondered what would have happened to the Hollywood icons, the great actors and actresses who had passed by our noses. What if they *hadn't* eventually gotten that pivotal part? Would they be behind a lunch counter somewhere asking, "Would you like fries with that?"

One day in 1987, while pondering this question as well as more universal ones (like what to schedule Friday nights at 8:00), I looked up from my desk to discover Joel Thurm, NBC's inspired casting guru. Joel had a devilish grin on his face.

"Are you busy?" he asked. "I've got something to show you. It'll only take a minute, but I guarantee it'll break your heart." How could I resist an offer like that?

Joel had undertaken a personal project at the network. He

was computerizing all of our audition tapes for easy access-
ing, and had, in the process, discovered a gold mine of "the
ones who got away."

As he loaded a tape into my VCR, he handed me a list of
the following names: Tom Cruise, Matthew Broderick, Meg
Ryan, Whitney Houston, Ally Sheedy, Dennis Quaid, Molly
Ringwald, and others almost as painful to mention.

While I was digesting this, he asked me if I remembered
Madonna ever reading for us. "No way," I said. "There's *no
way* Madonna could have slipped through our fingers."

But sure enough, he cued the tape, up came the clack-
board, and there was the Material Girl herself: sans blond
hair, but with that trademark attitude front and center. She
was reading for one of the female leads in the television series
Fame.

Years later, during my first meeting with Madonna at Paramount, I gave her my prized VHS of her audition. But not
before I played it for her.

She smiled, and said she had no bad feelings about that
audition.

I lied, and said neither did I.

SIX

....

Late Dates

What will you do when there's no more Johnny Carson?

If you were an executive at NBC at any time during the last thirty years, that was the one question you lived in fear of being asked.

When I arrived at the network in 1977, the joke around Hollywood was that NBC stood for Nothing But Carson. From my perspective, that was a little too true to be funny. NBC, back then, was third in prime-time ratings, third in daytime, and third in Saturday morning. *The Tonight Show* with Johnny Carson and a promising new venture called *Saturday Night Live* were the only things preventing us from becoming the fourth network before Fox was ever invented.

How important was Carson to NBC? Let's put it this way: His one show generated more profits than any NBC *division*, let alone any other NBC show. Johnny was also a symbol of NBC's role in television history: a link to a grand tradition of live, topical variety entertainment—to the NBC of Bob Hope, *Your Show of Shows*, Steve Allen, Dean Martin, Jack Paar, and Rowan and Martin. Because he'd been the *Tonight Show* host since 1962, Johnny didn't just continue the tradition; he now defined it.

You might think a star of that stature—and a man as personally complex as Johnny is—would be tough to manage. Far from it. Outside of a lone, much publicized contract dispute with Fred Silverman in the late seventies, Johnny was the Great Non-Squeaking Wheel at NBC. If you were head of the entertainment division, your work with Johnny was simple. All you had to do was keep him happy. And most of the time I did that by leaving him alone.

Johnny's contract called for the reverse of most Hollywood deals. He wanted it always to be *his* call whether or not to continue, so he chose to work on one-year options. Every January since 1988, he would announce whether or not he wanted his option renewed over lunch at a restaurant called the Grill in Beverly Hills. Although no real negotiating ever went on during those meetings, I would always be there with John Agoglia, NBC's executive vice president, and Johnny Carson always had his representative, Ed Hookstratten, at his side.

The meals were little rituals. Johnny knew that we were on pins and needles about the decision he was going to make, and so, being a compassionate guy, he'd never let us get past the soup or salad without signaling that he wanted to re-up for another year. Relaxed, we'd then spend the rest of the meal talking about such subjects as the latest pretenders to the late-night throne (Alan Thicke, Joan Rivers, Pat Sajak et al) or what was going on in the industry.

My last lunch with Johnny in 1991 was at the same locale, with the same people. But nothing else about it was business as usual. For one thing, it was delayed until late February as a result of my car accident. For another, the main course had been brought to the table and neither Agoglia nor I had gotten a sign from the King. Then suddenly we heard the words we didn't want to hear.

"Listen," Johnny said, "I think this year's going to be it. I can't do this forever. And there'll never be a perfect time to quit. So this is as good a time as any."

There was no arguing or pleading on our part. Johnny is a very resolute man, and there was no doubt about his certainty. The only thing left to ask about was a timetable.

"I'd like to leave by next September [of 1991]," Johnny said. His plan was to celebrate his thirtieth anniversary and sign off. Short notice to replace a legend.

The only person I brought into the loop during the next week was Bob Wright, the president and CEO of NBC. Together we decided that we should work for an extension, to push September as far into the future as possible. The subject of Johnny's replacement never came up. Neither of us wanted to think about the tough decisions that needed to be made in that regard.

First things first. I initiated a slew of phone calls to

Johnny—more in two weeks than I had made to him in the past two years. I asked him to reconsider his September deadline, not from the position of how his leaving affected NBC, but how it would affect his staff, many of whom had been with him since his move to the Coast in 1972. Those people, I said, would probably have a hard time finding work in the middle of a television season. He listened closely to what I was saying, and told me he'd think about it.

Then one day shortly thereafter Johnny called to ask if I would meet with him alone in his office on the floor below the *Tonight Show* set. I hung up the phone and went straight over.

He'd considered all the ramifications of his departure, he said, and he agreed to stay until the following May. I was glad for the staff members involved. I also was relieved for NBC; the network and its affiliates got two more sweeps periods (February and May) with Carson in command. Equally important, those extra few months would mean that NBC could now devote the June-to-September TV off-season to the task of promoting the person of choice, the new host of *The Tonight Show*.

I've always felt that Johnny was the show business equivalent of a world-class decathlete—maybe not the absolute best in the world in any one area (interviewing, monologues, sketch comedy) but great in a wide range of events. All of these qualities were in full evidence in his next to last show, when he traded quips with Robin Williams and sang "One More for the Road" with Bette Midler. For that night alone, as well as for the parade of great *Tonight Show* guests who dropped in during those final few months for one last visit, I'm happy Johnny pushed back his good-bye.

David Letterman is in several ways like Johnny Carson: He has the perfect instincts for a late-night talk-show host, he's Midwestern in attitude and demeanor—and he's extremely hard to know. I first met David when I arrived at NBC and he was getting set to do a one-hour morning show called, simply, *The David Letterman Show.* How did he behave at 10:00 A.M.? Exactly as he does after midnight. Letterman is Letterman, no matter what time he goes on the air. His morning show was a true howl from start to finish, but it was also—in terms of guests, tone, and general attitude—all wrong for the morning audience. At that hour viewers expect to see movie stars and authors chatting about their latest projects, lifestyle news, and features about cooking and fashion. David would have guests like former baseball player Bob Uecker talking about what it was like to watch a game from the bullpen.

The ratings were terrible right from the start. This led, as it always does in the land of TV, to a lot of meetings and discussions. At these meetings, Fred Silverman would often say things like, "Look, David, what I really want here is *The Arthur Godfrey Show.*" Every time Fred mentioned Godfrey, it was like that old Abbott and Costello routine—the one where the words "Niagara Falls" would cue one of the characters to get a crazed look in his eyes and say, "Slowly I turned . . ." My job would be to calm David down by telling him, "No, Fred doesn't want you to play the ukulele and talk to Julius

LaRosa. He's just talking about having a family of players and stuff like that. Don't worry. It'll be fine."

I lied. It wasn't close to fine. The show lasted four months.

Considering that David was being canceled for a couple of quiz shows—*High Rollers* and *Card Sharks*—he was pretty cool about it. On his final morning show, he even staged a moving "Tribute to Wink Martindale," the host of *High Rollers,* complete with a Rockettes-like chorus line of women wearing giant dice and playing cards. It was utterly hilarious—and exactly the kind of thing that is totally lost on 10:00 A.M. TV-watchers.

In the interim, Fred and I worked out a contract with Charlie Joffe, David's manager. Essentially, NBC paid David $1 million to take himself off the market. We felt David needed a vote of confidence. We also needed to buy some time to create an opportunity more suited to his talents. And we did, about a year later. The post-Carson time slot was perfect for David. But as is the way in scheduling, another problem arose: what to do with Tom Snyder's *Tomorrow Show.*

In the game of programming, when one show goes in, another gets moved or replaced. The *Tomorrow Show,* which had been on almost nine years at that point, was getting acceptable but not spectacular ratings following Carson. Still, I couldn't help but feel a twinge of regret about having to move *Tomorrow* back in the schedule. I'd grown fond of Tom, who had taken to calling Silverman and me Kramden and Norton. But Tom knew something wasn't jelling, either. He'd begun phoning me at home at night to complain about his then new cohost Rona Barrett. "Norton, wait till you see the show tonight," he'd say. "Wait till you hear what she said. It's

not working. It's *not working*. Listen, it's up to *you* to fix this."
In the end, the best approach to any difficult work situation
is to be honest and direct, and so the next time I was in New
York I called him and suggested that we talk about his future.

"Fine," Tom said. "Come by my town house. I've got a
great cook. And we can have privacy."

During lunch we talked at length about the Letterman
show, how I saw it filling a need in our schedule, and how its
comedy was more compatible with *The Tonight Show* than his
program was. Then, as we were leaving to go to work, I asked
Tom if he'd be willing to move to the 1:30 A.M. slot. He was
gracious but he said he didn't think so; that was simply too
late for people to be watching TV. (That hasn't proven to be
the case for Bob Costas, whose *Later* show is now sailing
profitably into its fifth year.)

"I've been on the air a long time, Brandon, and I can tell
you something," he said. "People watch my show. They really
like my show. The public," he said, "has a connection to Tom
Snyder."

At that point, Tom suggested that we take the relatively
short walk back to NBC. We'd gotten about a block when we
passed a construction site—where a chorus of hardhats spotted him. There was a lot of hooting and hollering, but that
didn't strike me as unusual; hardhats are the kind of guys
who'd razz Mother Teresa.

How did Tom react? He laughed that deep smoker's laugh
of his—"heh, heh, heh"—the trademark laugh made famous
by Dan Aykroyd doing his Snyder impersonation on *Saturday
Night Live.*

Tom eventually made a graceful exit from the tube, but not

from the business. He's got a nationally syndicated radio talk show these days, and he tells me he's never been happier.

Once *Late Night* started, David and I settled into a relationship of sorts. Basically, it worked like this: I would make suggestions, and he would ignore them. Since one of my earliest suggestions was that he should have Don King, the boxing promoter, as an Ed McMahon–type sidekick, ignoring me had its rewards. (Sometimes he listened, though. For years, the two of us hashed around the idea of bringing back Howdy Doody via the Letterman writers. That idea finally fell through when Paul Shaffer didn't want to don the buckskins to become Buffalo Paul.)

I've always found myself drawn toward David's twisted sense of comedy. Because of that, a lot of people ask me why I didn't pick him to replace Johnny Carson.

What I tell them is this: *I* didn't pick anyone to replace Johnny Carson.

By the time that difficult decision had to be made, I was already a lame duck, a few months away from starting my job at Paramount. Thus, the decision I dreaded having to make fell to Bob Wright, Warren Littlefield, and Rick Ludwin, the head of late-night programming. I didn't envy them. It was an extremely tough call for anyone to make, a choice between the two guys at NBC who both could do the job—and who both deserved it.

Jay Leno and David Letterman had worked hard to shape and refine their very different TV personas. Jay is the Dutiful Son, always respectful of his guests and careful not to alienate the old Carson audience. He's clearly the best monologuist of the three late-night contenders; he's getting better at interviewing, at relaxing, and simply being himself. Jay is America's hardest-working comedian, and he campaigned skillfully for the job of *Tonight Show* host, visiting local affiliates whenever he was on the road, and taping promos and making appearances for them whenever he could. Jay has done well despite having a considerable challenge: He is the only host in late night who didn't invent the format for his show. He inherited it from someone else.

Letterman is Peck's Bad Boy, always looking to stir up trouble and daring the older, mainstream viewers to stay with him. He's never been a great interviewer, but he makes up for it with his unpretentious, free-for-all style of comedy.

Of course, the Leno-Letterman debate isn't my problem anymore. In moving to Paramount, I've become coach of the Arsenio Hall team. I feel a little bit like Pat Riley going from the Lakers to the Knicks and then having to play his own guys.

Except that I go pretty far back with Arsenio, too. I've known him since he was a writer and an occasional performer on an NBC summer series we did in the mid-eighties called *Motown Revue.* What was impressive about him then, and even more so now, is his pure show-biz smarts. Like Leno and Letterman, Arsenio has his persona, too: He's the Smart, Funny Guy in the Back of the Class, the ringleader who gets you to go along with him on his late-night escapades. He knows his audience and his abilities as a performer, and that's a powerful combination. I think Arsenio will get an even larger following as he matures and mellows as a TV personality. He's the youngest of the three late-night princes, and therefore his potential is perhaps the greatest.

Of course, I still haven't told you how I would have settled the Leno-Letterman debate had I still been in charge. Let me put it this way. The safer move was to Jay because the sales department and the affiliates preferred him. He could keep more of Carson's audience as well as attract younger viewers. In addition, with Jay the network would know exactly what it was getting, since he had done a fabulous job of being the exclusive guest host for five years. Those are all very good reasons for casting your lot with Leno. But the inveterate gambler in me would also have been curious about what unpredictable lunacy Letterman would have brought to the party—what he might be inspired to do if he finally got the job he'd waited ten years for.

On a close call like this, many factors come into play. How was the new fall 1991 schedule being received? (Remember, I hadn't selected the shows or put together that schedule.) How real were the rumors that Leno would go to CBS if he didn't get the nod? (Since the decision wasn't mine, I didn't check.) If the schedule had been going great, and if the rumors weren't real, I would have seriously considered the relatively risky move of slotting in Letterman an hour earlier.

Until a clear winner emerges, it's going to be fun watching the competition these next few years.

Whoever emerges the winner, though, the last great ride in late night television will always belong to John W. Carson.

SEVEN

....

Sharks in
Lake Michigan

Ⅰn the late seventies, some ABC executives caused quite a scandal when word got out that they were consulting with psychic Beverly Dean on important programming decisions. I've never gone to that kind of an extreme for help in decoding the vagaries of America's television audience, though believe me, I understand the impulse. I personally had it once when I encountered a palm reader at a birthday party for Bob Hope's daughter Linda.

"So," I said to the palmist. "What can you tell me about myself?"

"Ah," he said, staring at my hand. "The company you work

for isn't doing so well, but you yourself are in line for advancement."

"Hey, that's pretty good," I said. "Right now I'm sweating out a promotion."

"Oh, really?" he said. "Where do you work?"

"NBC," I said. "I'm the director of comedy development."

"*You* work at NBC?"

"Yeah, why?"

"*I* used to work at NBC. In advertising design. Things got slow and I got laid off. Now I'm doing this psychic stuff."

My faith in the occult was permanently shaken. Still, as I said, I understand the impulse to resort to cosmic solutions in the television business, and never more than when you're trying to figure out the audience. No entertainment executive is anything more than a highly paid slave to the audience. That's the first rule of show business: The audience is your lord and master. What's strange is that the greatest challenge in show business is to figure out who the audience *is*. And there's no one easy answer. The audience is like a glacier—a massive entity that only *seems* to be standing still but in reality keeps moving, changing, fragmenting, and reconfiguring in unexpected ways. In the movie business, the only audience standing still is the audience in line at the box office—and they're even more uncertain, because they're not just spending their time, they're spending their money. When I was at NBC, I used to tell people that creating the new fall schedule was like shopping for Sybil, the woman with the multiple personalities—and you can never predict with any certainty which one of them is going to show up every night to watch your programs.

In order to tell you about my lifelong search for the audience, I have to take you back to the summer I spent in the dark.

After prep school (Lawrenceville, in New Jersey) and before college (Yale), I worked as an usher at the Alhambra Theater in San Francisco, the city where my folks had moved a few years earlier. There wasn't much for me to do except to watch the movie, and then—after I'd done that about four or five times—to watch the audience watch the movie. I'd take note of when they were laughing, when they were moved to cry, or when they were restless and bored enough to get up for popcorn. I also noticed that there were certain kinds of jokes and dramatic devices that didn't appeal to me personally, yet always drew a strong and consistent reaction.

Funny how life works out. Today I'm running a movie studio and I go to as many theater screenings as possible. I still learn things from how an audience reacts, and what I learn can sometimes help the producers and directors of our films. When I was a teenager I watched the audience to keep from going crazy. Now I watch them to stay employed.

How do you know if you're connecting with the audience? Well, the Nielsen ratings are the traditional means of measuring your success—just like the box office is for movie executives—but there *are* other methods. Preston Beckman, an associate of mine at NBC, used to take his dog for walks around his Westchester, New York, neighborhood and peer in peoples' windows to see what they were watching. Preston swore his method was just as effective as Nielsen's. The scary thing was that he became one of the senior vice presidents of research at NBC. Preston actually used to worry that we were going to make important programming decisions before he was able to walk his dog one more time. I, on the other hand, used to worry that we'd come in one morning and find out that he didn't even own a dog and had been arrested as a Peeping Tom.

So why, with all the sophisticated research facilities a network has at its disposal, is it still so difficult to get a grip?

Consider the TV series *Walking Tall*. We were in the dawn of the Reagan administration, Carter was out, and according to our new president, it was morning in America—remember? Rarely has the nation gone through such a dramatic mood swing. And seldom have I found myself standing by with a show that seemed so custom-built for the times.

Walking Tall was an hour-long crime drama based on a series of fairly successful movies about real-life sheriff Buford Pusser, a cult hero who cut through all the liberal hogwash and meted out justice swiftly, and with a club. So the show was an instant smash, right? Wrong. The series premiered around Inauguration Day, and by summer it was as much a piece of trivia as Billy Beer. Watching *Walking Tall* belly flop was professionally painful for me, but at least I learned something: There's a totally different dynamic at work when people are pulling levers in a voting booth from when they're selecting channels on their TV sets. The former is motivated by fear; the latter is motivated by pleasure.

By 1990, Reagan was gone, George Bush had arrived—and ABC was about to air something called *Twin Peaks*. The show, as you probably recall, was a weird mixture of murder, adultery, pie-eating, and a dancing dwarf. It premiered at 9:00 P.M. on Easter Sunday—a time slot that the NBC network had

traditionally reserved for entertainment appropriate for rev-
erential holidays: Franco Zeffirelli's *Jesus of Nazareth.* I knew
I was in trouble when I came home that night and found our
nanny, a devout Catholic, watching David Lynch's Log Lady.
Of course, *Twin Peaks* became a cultural phenomenon. People didn't just tune in once a week; they talked about it at the
breakfast table and around the fax machine at work. The
media, moreover, leveled entire forests for the purpose of
writing prose in praise of this daring and bent series.

How worried was I about *Twin Peaks* madness? Very. *Twin
Peaks*'s regular time slot was directly opposite the heart of the
NBC lineup: 9:00 P.M. Thursday, smack-dab against *Cheers.*
Whatever they would get would surely come out of our hide.
Not only was the show disconcertingly different, but so was its
creator. The day after the premiere, Lilly and Calla were
going back to L.A. from New York, and Lilly noticed David
Lynch sitting across the aisle from her on the plane. "Excuse
me," she said to him, in her inimitably straightforward fashion, "but I just want to say that Brandon Tartikoff is my
husband, and you're making him absolutely miserable. By the
way, congratulations on your ratings."

Lynch seemed somewhat bewildered. "Ratings?"

Lilly said, "You know, because your show got a thirty-five
share last night."

"Oh, it did?" Lynch said.

There it was nearly ten o'clock in the morning, and he
hadn't called in for the overnights.

"Lilly," I said, when she told me that story, "what producer
who wants to stay in business doesn't call in for the ratings?
He's even more dangerous than I thought."

And yet, after all is said and done, *Twin Peaks* cannot be considered a major hit; it stayed on the air only slightly longer than *Walking Tall.* To my mind, Lynch and his coproducer, Mark Frost, were like weekend fishermen who, when they tossed their lines into the water, hooked Jaws. But they couldn't hold on to that big a fish. The episodes kept meandering along, teasing viewers with portentous "clues" but never providing any real payoff. In a matter of months, only hard-core fans and the fringe media were still caught up in the show. *Twin Peaks* madness had completely subsided.

When I got my first network job, in the mid-1970s, the business was still being run by the executives who had pioneered the medium of television. Men and women who could remember a time in their own lives when there was no television, and whose childhood memories and formative experiences were closely connected with the age of radio. Many of them were the minds that had shaped the original Golden Age of Television in the 1950s. I'll always be in awe of and in debt to them. And yet, being from the next generation gave me a distinct advantage; it was probably the main reason I was able to rise quickly through the ranks and become president of NBC's entertainment division at the age of thirty-one. Even though they were brilliant at what they did, those older guys were, in the end, always *guessing* what the postradio generation wanted. I was the audience we wanted to reach, and I simply had to look only as far as the mirror or my own peer group to figure out what they would watch.

I was a child of television. Growing up in suburban Freeport, Long Island, I watched *Father Knows Best, Howdy Doody,*

The Twilight Zone, Ernie Kovacs, The Fugitive, Dobie Gillis, Bonanza, and (when I was home sick from school) *I Married Joan* and *My Little Margie.* To go with my ten-sitcoms-a-day TV habit I even had a perfectly symmetrical 1950s sitcom family: one father (Jordan, a clothing manufacturer), one mother (Enid, a marketing exec), one sister (Lisa)—and one seven-inch black-and-white DuMont TV set, around which we all gathered, Cleaverishly. My parents got along fine. While we weren't rich, we weren't deprived, either. My sister and I went to summer camp, got braces, and ate out at a Chinese restaurant every Sunday. I had a swell bicycle. I have never been to a shrink.

I wanted to mention all this so there would finally be one book on the market that people could close with a smile and say, "My God, this man is in *total denial.*"

Once, when I was a kid, I turned to my mother during an episode of *Dennis the Menace* and said, "They've really ruined this show. Jay North isn't the right kid to play Dennis. He's too goody-goody." Thirty-some years later, I stand by that opinion. But I never actually thought about TV as a profession until my senior year at college. The year before, I had switched majors—from economics to English. This change was motivated by both my enduring love of the language and my getting drunk while watching Joe Namath's Jets whip the Colts in Super Bowl III; I failed the next day's macroeconomics final.

In any case, my destiny was suggested during a writing seminar conducted by the distinguished and Pulitzer Prize–winning novelist Robert Penn Warren. It was a quiet midweek afternoon, and we were discussing a D. H. Lawrence short story. When I happened to mention that I thought the plot would work better if one of the character's sisters had been his girlfriend, Penn Warren took off his glasses, looked me in the eye, and said, "Young man, have you ever considered a career in television?"

This was the tail end of the sixties, so, in keeping with the fashion of the times, I wasn't thinking much about a career in *anything*. Still, Penn Warren's remark resonated, and a few months later, I was standing in front of WTNH, the ABC affiliate in New Haven. I was about to have my first real encounter with the medium, and I am where I am today in spite of what happened then.

My basic problem as I set out to get a job in television, freshly typed script tucked under my arm, was that, for all the hours I'd spent unlearning the great literature I'd learned at Yale and basking in front of the cathode-ray tube, I had no idea of how the TV business worked. The way I saw it, I had a TV show to sell. So why should I travel eighty miles to New York and pay for parking and tolls when there was a TV *station* right in New Haven?

"Wait till you hear this," I actually said as I sat down across the desk from David Wilson, the WTNH program manager. "I'm going to make your day." Then I presented him with *George and Martha*. This was a soap-opera parody that I had written as a class assignment and rehearsed with some members of the Yale Drama School. "I'll write all the episodes, I'll provide the actors—all we need is a living-room set," I said. "It'll be great." One could possibly say that *George and Martha* was ahead of its time; five years later, Norman Lear would do a similar concept called *Mary Hartman, Mary Hartman* that would have a successful run in syndication. But in 1970, the project spoke mostly of my intriguing blend of arrogance and stupidity.

To this day, I'm impressed with David Wilson's patience. He didn't simply throw me out. For one thing, he took the time to explain that local stations such as WTNH didn't create their own entertainment; they ran network programs, bought syndicated shows, and provided local news and public-affairs programming.

For another thing, he informed me that the TV audience was not exactly symbolized by me and my Yalie friends.

"Do you have an Instamatic camera?" Wilson asked me.

"Uh, no, but I suppose I could get one."

"Well, when you do, go down to the Port Authority terminal in New York City," he said. "Then take a picture of the first hundred people you see get off the buses. Have those pictures blown up to eight-by-ten glossies, and wherever you go to work in television, put the photographs on the wall. And every time you make a programming decision, look at those pictures and ask yourself, Will *they* like it? If you do that, you'll be very successful in this business."

You can graduate from college with a degree in broadcasting and never get advice that sound. But Dave Wilson passed it along freely. And *then* he threw me out.

I don't usually keep in touch with those who've reduced me to quivering jelly, but for the next year, while I hung around New Haven working as a copywriter at a local ad agency, I stayed in touch with Wilson. Maybe one of these days he'll have a job for me, I thought. And then, one of those days, he did. Wilson was leaving to work in Philadelphia, someone was moving up to take his place, and that left an entry-level opening in the promotion department. It was a step down, salarywise, from the ad-agency job, but that didn't matter. I was getting to work in television. I would have paid them.

One day Malcolm Potter, Wilson's replacement as the director of programming, asked me if I wanted to go along with him to visit the Beltsville, Maryland, headquarters of Arbitron, the company responsible for the ratings of the local TV shows. He was going to inspect the viewer logs in which people in the New Haven–Hartford area had been recording the shows they'd watched for the past several weeks. That meant I'd be sitting in a cement-walled storage room and paging through about 1,200 booklets.

I loved every minute of it.

Knowing the ratings we were getting was fine, but by this time I'd had enough of a sip to want to get beyond the statistics and look at the *way* the audience recorded their viewing habits. Did they, for example, take the time to write in the shows they watched every night, the way they were supposed to? Judging by the handwriting, it seemed not. It seemed like they got bored with their homework assignment over the weekend and then on Tuesday, the last night of the rating week, filled out the logs in a rush. And it seemed that they were claiming, in the case of the local news broadcasts, to have watched all week what they'd watched only on that final evening. After my day at Arbitron, I concentrated on promoting our Tuesday news broadcasts. Owing to human behavior (read laziness), it seemed that the station that won on Tuesday night would handily win the local news battle for the week.

At a smaller station you may not get to work on the biggest, hottest shows, but you do get to learn about the audience. In a smaller market you walk the streets with the people you're programming for; you take their calls on the phone-in shows and you answer the viewer mail. Besides that, the people at WTNH were always generous with their knowledge and time. I learned everything from film and tape editing to how to write news stories and even how to direct.

The latter opportunity arose often, on Saturday nights. That was when our little station resembled an episode of the old *Mary Tyler Moore Show* as directed by that master of despair Ingmar Bergman. To begin, the director of our late-news show would get falling-down drunk, and I'd have to do his job. This meant spending six hours in a control room that had the ambience of the Führer's bunker. Keeping me company were a surly, overweight audio engineer and an overweight, surly cameraman. The company was bad enough, but when I'd check the network feed coming in from ABC to find relief there, on the monitor would be some of the absolute worst shows in television history. I'm talking about *Getting Together* with Bobby Sherman, *The Persuaders* with Tony Curtis, *Shirley's World* with Shirley MacLaine. "I can do that," I began mumbling to myself. Unfortunately, I was usually in the middle of producing a *Lassie* promo, so not even the audio engineer could hear me.

Eventually I escaped, although things didn't work out as I'd planned. I wanted to move immediately to a job at the ABC offices in Los Angeles, and so every few months I'd weigh my suitcase down with a manhole-size master reel of videotape (this was the pre-cassette era) and fly out to California to do a round of job interviews. The tapes contained examples of my work: commercials for our news team; comedy sketches written by me and performed by some local radio personalities moonlighting as actors; promos for everything from our afternoon movies to *Donahue* to syndicated programs like *Lawrence Welk* and *You Asked for It.*

I thought this video résumé would help me land a job as a writer for network promos that could lead to a job on, say, *The Sonny and Cher Comedy Hour.* On a trip out West I called on Harry Marks, who thought differently. Harry was ABC's head of promotions on the West Coast and probably the only network executive who actually took the time to look at my audition reel. "This is the single worst piece of crap I've ever seen," he told me. "Your film is dirty and scratched, the editing is atrocious, and we've got a new thing out here—it's called pacing. If you entertain any hopes of making it in Hollywood, please don't show this to anyone ever again."

My ego was crushed. But his response prompted me to clean up my act and improve my reel considerably. The next year I assaulted San Francisco, talking to some people at KGO-TV the ABC-owned station there. They had no jobs to offer, but they did know of an opening for an assistant promotions manager at their sister station, WLS in Chicago. It wasn't *Sonny and Cher,* but hey, how many things in life are?

Chicago turned out to be the classroom that New Haven never quite was. I was now in the third-largest market in the country. A-list movie stars dropped into Chicago talk shows when they had something to sell, as did your best-selling authors. The network paid attention to us, we had some money to work with, and the people at the station were, for the most part, consummate pros. I figured I was lucky to be working at WLS at the age of twenty-four. I also figured that if I was stuck in Chicago for more than two years, I would kill myself.

I was looking for someone to lead me out of the wilderness to the promised land. Who would serve as my guide? None other than the audience.

One day, not long after I arrived at WLS, I happened to notice that something strange occurred when we ran *Cotton Comes to Harlem* as the 3:30 movie. This was the fourth or fifth time the movie had run, but this time the ratings leaped by 50 percent. Overnight Nielsen meters had just been installed in the market a few months before, and we were very excited about the possibilities of instant feedback from the audience, but we'd never seen anything quite *this* dramatic.

So up the hall I went to see Lew Erlicht, then the station manager, to ask if, just for the hell of it, we could run *Buck and the Preacher* with Sidney Poitier in the same time slot the next week. He shrugged and said, "Go for it." And the ratings, once again, went through the roof.

I went back to Lew, waving the ratings printouts and claiming the greatest discovery since Jonas Salk. Lew would be my rival at ABC about eight years later, when we were both heads of programming for our respective networks—but right now we were on the same side, and I knew he shared my competitive instincts. "I think we're onto something here," I said. "I think there's a black bias in the audience sample. I don't know how it happened, but it seems like Nielsen has got a disproportionate number of black households wired. Let's

milk the library for that audience and run up the score." Lew
liked the idea, and for the next six weeks we ran black-ori-
ented sitcoms, movies with black actors, and special reports
on the South Side of Chicago as part of the Eyewitness news-
casts. Some of our viewers, black and white, may have been
mystified, especially after we showed the seventh run of *A
Raisin in the Sun* in the February sweeps, but we cleaned up
in the ratings—until the Nielsen folks caught on and got a
new sample of viewers.

To some that may sound like a cynical attempt to manipu-
late the system. So let me say this: You're right; it *was*. The
ratings game is just that: a game. And as long as I was playing,
and each ratings point meant millions of dollars annually, I
was going to play to win.

Gee, but I sound like a Force to Reckon With, no? The fact
is, I had the drive and the dream but, in reality, none of the
power. How low did I, as assistant promo manager, rank in
the station hierarchy? So low that when Bob Kennedy, the
morning talk-show host at WLS, asked if he could use my
body for an on-the-air scientific experiment, there was no way
I could refuse.

Bob wanted me for his special New Year's Eve morning
broadcast. The idea was that I would spend from 7:00 to 7:58
A.M. getting drunk, and the remaining two minutes submit-
ting to a Breathalyzer test administered by a Chicago cop. I
guess we were trying to demonstrate that drinking results in
drunkenness—which leads in turn to drunk driving. Or something. In any case, I agreed to go along.

I sat with the other morning-show guests and downed gin
and tonics until I got the distinct feeling that I could lick

anybody in the greenroom. Unfortunately, the only people there (besides me and the Chicago cop) were a team of husband and wife puppeteers, and Pat Loud and her daughter, who were there to promote a book. The Louds had just done a controversial documentary on PBS where a camera crew spent a year in their "typical American household." "Geez, they're dressed like a couple of circus clowns," I observed, after drink four. My memory has been muddied by the gin-and-tonic haze I was in, but I vaguely recall Mrs. Loud lunging at me from across the room. If the cop hadn't been there, I might not be around to tell this thrilling tale.

After I had the sixth drink, I could hardly walk. Then they brought me out onstage and administered the Breathalyzer test. The result, according to the test, was that I was sober. Perfectly fine to drive. As the credits rolled, I sat there pie-eyed while the cop mumbled about how the machine had to be on for an hour, he guessed, before it worked. All in all, another Great Moment in Television.

Screwups were a part of life at a local station. Thus it was that Lew Erlicht came by my office one day and asked me to look at some film the news department had shot at great expense. The movie *Jaws* had just come out, and in an attempt to capitalize on its success, we had sent our anchorman down to the Caribbean to do a five-part series on sharks. What he came back with, though, was a total bust. All we had was seemingly endless footage of the anchorman sitting in a boat and talking while, off to the side, a gray mass would loom up in the water, then disappear. I remember sitting in the screening room and thinking, There's no way out of this mess. We've spent most of the news department's budget for the quarter, we've hyped it on the air, and now there's nothing we can use.

"This isn't even good Jacques Cousteau," Lew said. "What we need's a little Hollywood."

I sighed. Then it hit me: We had *a lot* of Hollywood, down in the station's movie vaults. About an hour later, I was in the editing bay with our own news footage and a lurid documentary called *Blue Water, White Death.* I don't know much about editing, but I know what I spliced: Basically, our anchorman's voice went in over scenes of sharks roiling the water and attacking divers. After I laid a little *Jaws* music on the sound track, it seemed, at some level, to work. Of course, this was an absolute TV no-no. Mixing movies and news footage—even if the intent was not deception (we credited the movie)—was totally against the rules. I'm glad I didn't know about that at the time, or I might never have done it. As Paul McCartney once said about the Beatles, "Our career was helped immeasurably by the fact that we couldn't read music."

Our ad-agency people were playing a little fast and loose themselves. The artwork they came up with was a blatant rip-off of the *Jaws* campaign—lone swimmer on the surface; huge shark loitering below. "*Sharks,*" the copy said, "*Eyewitness News.* Five Parts This Week." I couldn't wait to show it to Lew, who was fond of saying things like "Hearst was right— you can fool 'em every day." I imagined him clapping me on the back and saying, "Good work, kid. This'll really get 'em." What he actually did, though, was squint at the ad awhile, then say we didn't go far enough.

"I want the skyline of Chicago put in behind the water," he

said, waving his hand at the sketch. "I want to see the Hancock Building."

"But, Lew," I said. "There are no sharks in Lake Michigan."

"I don't give a shit," he said. "Put Chicago in there."

Lew smelled blood, and while protesting every step of the way, the agency art director redesigned the ad to Lew's specifications. And for that week, a news broadcast that had been getting between a 6 and a 7 in the ratings took a wild leap to 15.

Meanwhile, I continued to do anything that might help me land a better job. I made sure to introduce myself to every ABC executive who ever visited the station, who ever *considered* visiting the station, or whose travel plans called for him to change planes in O'Hare. And when all else failed, as it usually did, I begged for attention from itinerant celebrities. Then one day while I was fluctuating somewhere between gloom and frustration, it happened. Lew walked in my office and presented me with a first-class one-way ticket out. I'm speaking figuratively here. What he did in reality was ask me if I could create a commercial attesting to the uncanny accuracy of our weatherman, John Coleman. My imagination took over from there. I figured, "Yeah, I'll just do the greatest commercial in the history of thirty-second weather promo spots. Then I'll make sure some ABC honcho sees how I can write and produce. And I'll be out of here like *that*."

The spot I envisioned called for a split-screen effect. Coleman would be on one side, fiddling with his sun symbols and rain clouds; a magician performing classic nightclub tricks would be on the other. "People always ask me how I do what I do," the magician would say. "But what *I* want to know is, how does John Coleman predict the weather so accurately, day in and day out?" Then the magician would remove his hat, pull out a rabbit, and say, "John, I take my hat off to you. I don't know how you do it." Cool, huh?

I put out a casting call, and I imagined that a few days later all sorts of exotic men in shiny tuxedos and long black capes would crowd into the reception area near my office. In reality, about a half-dozen rather ordinary-looking guys showed up. The first five were pretty much the same: They pulled scarves out of their mouths, they did the sleight-of-hand card routines—and they all said the rabbit trick couldn't be performed as written. The kind of hat you pull a rabbit from, they explained, has a secret compartment that makes the hat too small to put on your head. I was about to give up—and then in walked magician number six. His name, he said, was the Great Pascou, and the rabbit trick, he assured me, was no problem. "Hey, I've pulled rabbits out of hats all over America," he said. "I've worked on Broadway."

Broadway—I realized on the day of the actual shoot—is a very long street.

The Great Pascou arrived, bowed deeply in my direction—and then proceeded to burn both his hands badly while rehearsing the fire-shoots-out-of-fingers trick. Stagehands rushed to his aid with fire extinguishers and Vaseline. So now we had a magician with sore, greasy fingers, and for the rest of the day, rings and coins squirted out of his control. Endless retakes were necessary. Of course, Pascou couldn't fit the hat with the rabbit on *his* head, either, and we had to resort to camera tricks to get something we could use. I was disgusted. When it was over all I wanted to do was forget the whole thing. Then, about a month later, the Great Pascou called me.

"I just wanted to thank you one more time before I left for the Coast," he said.

"The Coast?"

"Yeah," he said. "An ABC executive happened to catch the commercial. He was putting together a special on magic, and now he wants to use me on the show. This is my big break, and I owe it all to you. I'm on my way to Hollywood right now." A jet engine roared in the background, right on cue.

For a moment, I was speechless. Then I said, "Hey, listen, break a leg."

I meant it, too. With all my heart.

As educational as they were, however, it wasn't the bad experiences that kept me going. It was the occasional successes—the times when I was permitted to exercise some judgment, and then see that judgment vindicated by the Greater Chicago–area viewing public. I am talking here about the single greatest triumph I ever achieved at WLS: "Gorilla My Dreams Week" on the good old three-thirty *Afternoon Movie.*

I've always had a thing for monkey movies—everything from *Bedtime for Bonzo* to *Mighty Joe Young.* One day I did a computer search and found out that WLS owned a dozen films in which simians played a prominent part. I pulled five of those gorilla thrillas, including such classics as *King Kong* and *Planet of the Apes,* and spent three hundred dollars on a thirty-second promo in which a guy in a gorilla suit holding a ten-foot-high banana crooned special lyrics to "Gorilla My Dreams." He wore a top hat similar to Pascou's, and the only thing he burned was the competition. Thanks to this camp commercial, that week of movies averaged an 18 rating, up from a previous high of 8. The jump was so great that it came to the attention of Fred Silverman, head of the network. Buoyed by that success, I came right back with a "Week of Evil." We showed *Garden of Evil, See No Evil,* and even *Evel Knievel*—hey, what the hell, I was on a roll.

Fade out/fade in. I am walking nervously into the executive offices at ABC's headquarters on New York's Avenue of the Americas to have an audience (that's the only way to put it) with Fred Silverman. I've just spent the entire flight from Chicago trying to memorize the network's prime-time schedule by reading, and rereading, a copy of *TV Guide.* It was the only way I could think of to prepare for a meeting with a true TV legend.

Fred, who's obviously been briefed on what I've been up to, puts me at ease immediately. "You know," he says as I take a seat, "you remind me of me."

He doesn't elaborate, but from reading *Television: The Business Behind the Box,* I know what he means. I had done "Gorilla My Dreams Week"; *he,* fifteen years earlier on Chicago's WGN, had repackaged a bunch of grade-Z Tarzan-type flicks as a new show called *Bomba the Jungle Boy*—and made a bundle for his station. I guess it was a bond, of sorts.

I sensed immediately from Fred's attitude that he was

going to try to find a job for me someplace at ABC. So I allowed myself to relax, and to soak up the moment.

"You know how I got out of Chicago?" Fred said, obviously warming to the memory. "I was driving down North Lake Shore Drive one morning when it was about ten below with the windchill factor, and my car broke down. I sat there for a minute thinking about the situation. Then I got out, threw my keys in the front seat, caught a cab to the airport, and took a plane to New York. I found a job there, and I never looked back."

Fred paused a moment. Then he looked across his desk at me.

"Now *you* want to get out of Chicago."

Fade out/fade in. It's five months later, and I am in Los Angeles, where, thanks to Fred, I have a fairly low-level job as a "manager of dramatic development" for ABC. On this particular night, however, I'm attending my first real Hollywood function: the premiere of the movie *Network*. Searchlights scan the sky above the MGM lot, where the screening is being held. A seemingly endless stream of limos line up outside the theater. Somewhere between the car carrying Faye Dunaway and the one with William Holden am I, driving what for all practical purposes could be the very car that Fred Silverman had abandoned on North Lake Shore Drive. The body is rusted out, and I've got a first base from my old softball league wedged into what's left of the floorboards. But do I care? I'm twenty-seven, I've been in town two weeks, and everywhere I look there are familiar faces. Faces I'd met on my television screen while growing up.

The movie itself blew me away. Paddy Chayefsky had written a screenplay that made *Network* more than mere entertainment. Here was a scathingly funny (and sometimes depressingly dead-on) story of TV executives who'd sold their souls for ratings. Dunaway especially was superb as the crazed career woman who suffered from the female equivalent of premature ejaculation. I thought it was one of the most provocative and compelling movies I'd ever seen. Critics who later reviewed the movie accused Chayefsky of hyperbole. From where I sat, he treated television with understatement. My only question was how this theater full of TV people would react to such a searing indictment of themselves and their industry. By the time the film was on its last reel, I felt sure that MGM couldn't possibly go through with the "gala" party that was scheduled to take place behind the theater. When the lights came on, though, the crowd drifted in that direction, and I went along.

The first person I saw in the party tent was an executive I knew from ABC. "Gee," I said to him, "what did you think of that movie?"

His answer was swift. "It'll do okay in New York and L.A.," he said, "but it'll die in the sticks."

I was still mulling over his response when I got on the buffet line—and realized I was standing behind Danny Thomas, a man whom I'd considered a font of fatherly wisdom ever since I first watched him on *Make Room for Daddy*. A crony was asking him how he liked the picture.

"Paddy, Paddy, Paddy," he was saying, as he stood there with his cigar in one hand, and a plate of food in the other. "Paddy, Paddy, Paddy, Paddy, Paddy."

That was *his* take on the movie.

I had some cheese, drank some wine, and then decided it was time to go. Walking across the MGM lot (now the Sony lot), I saw a woman who'd once been a high-powered executive at NBC and who had shaken things up there with her aggressive style. She was storming toward her car and screaming, "I'm gonna fucking sue! That Faye Dunaway character was *me*! I'm gonna call my lawyer at nine o'clock in the morning and sue their fucking asses off!"

The man she was with was trying to calm her down. "Aw, c'mon, babe," he said. "That can't be you. You don't come *that* quick."

I stood there and watched their car drive off, and a thought occurred to me: I have just seen a Paddy Chayefsky movie.

And now I was *living* one.

EIGHT

Not Your Typical Nine-to-Five Job

I t is five P.M., and I have just spent the past hour in Frank Zappa's living room listening to him pitch me an idea for a TV show. Normally I don't make house calls, but then, normally Frank Zappa does not phone. If you're from my generation and a legendary rock star invites you over, you don't stand on show-business protocol. You get in your car and you go. But first you grab a witness.

Zappa lives in a weird-looking windmill-shaped house high up on Mulholland Drive. Warren Littlefield and I arrived at 4:00, and at 4:03 we were sitting in Frank's living room, holding bottles of Rolling Rock and listening to him describe how the industry we represented had thoroughly screwed up American society.

Frank said that people who came of age in the fifties got bombarded with perfect TV mothers like Donna Reed, and perfect TV fathers like Hugh Beaumont on *Leave It to Beaver*. That, according to Frank, made everyone dissatisfied with their own imperfect families, and caused "the whole Vietnam thing," the "Me Generation," and the Yuppies. "I look at TV as a virus," he said somberly. "I can cure it. But to do that, I have to get inside the tube."

Which led him into a pitch for a series called *The Zappa Family Comedy*.

He wasn't kidding about the family part. His fourteen-year-old son, Dweezil, came out and sang an "anti–Mother's Day song." His sixteen-year-old daughter, Moon Unit, had a great idea for some fantasy sequences for her part of the show. "I always liked that cartoon *Josie and the Pussycats* when I was growing up," she said, "and I was thinking, why not do a live-action version of that?"

"Mmmm," I said. "Yes." An all-girl rock group solving crimes in outer space did not exactly strike me as what America was waiting for. But we thanked her for her thoughts—we thanked them profusely for all their thoughts—and Warren and I rushed back to the office.

Nothing ever came of that visit—although Dweezil and Moon Unit wound up doing a short-lived series for CBS called *Normal Life*.

Still, it wasn't a waste of time for us—or Zappa—by any means. We got to dine out on the fact that we'd been to Frank Zappa's house. And he got to tell people that two top network programmers had come over to hear his kids pitch a TV show.

In baseball they call that a perfect trade.

Our fairy tale begins when a small regional toy company visits Phyllis Tucker Vinson, NBC's head of Saturday morning programming in the eighties. They pitch her an idea for a kids' cartoon. One that would feature a chubby, moon-faced character based on the prototype of a doll they were developing. The deal is, if we take the cartoon, we can, for little money, get an ownership position in the doll's sales.

"What do you think?" Phyllis asked, handing me the prototype.

"Well, why don't I take it home and see how my daughter likes it?"

That night, I placed the doll in Calla's crib. Since she was not much more than a year old at the time, I wasn't expecting a detailed reaction. The one I got, however, came from someone else. My mother-in-law. When she discovered the doll in the crib, she grabbed it and flung it into the hall closet. "Why did you put that thing in the crib with the baby?"

"Well," I started to say, "you see, that's the first model of a brand-new doll—"

"I don't really care," she interrupted. "*Just keep it away from Calla.* It's the ugliest thing I've ever seen. You're going to scare her to death. You'll give her nightmares."

The next day, Phyllis asked me if I'd given any more thought to making the deal on the doll and the accompanying cartoon series.

"Forget it," I said, my mother-in-law's voice still ringing in my ears. "It'll never work. Kids'll be afraid to play with it."

End of fairy tale? Not quite. The investment we passed on turned out to be worth a few bucks. A company called Coleco stepped in and made $150 million the next year. You may have heard of the doll. Its name is Cabbage Patch.

A network boardroom resembles a government war room. All the generals assemble to devise the strategies that determine who wins the ratings war and who becomes its prisoner.

This day, a sub-zero Sunday afternoon in 1978, the generals gathered on the fifth floor of 30 Rockefeller Center. The key members of the Silverman Cabinet ringed the conference table, dressed in an assortment of relaxed winter casual. We had been summoned by Fred that morning, prompted by the continued dismal weekend ratings. Fridays were a disaster, due to the surging dominance of CBS's *Dallas;* Saturdays were a toxic-waste dump, due to ABC's *The Love Boat.*

So there we were: Bob Mulholland, the head of the network; Irwin Segelstein, the executive vice president of NBC; Bob Butler, the head of finance; Ray Timothy, the head of affiliate relations; Bill Reubens, the head of research; and me—the whipping boy, the lucky person in charge of prime-time production.

Everyone's attention was fixated on Fred's programming board. It had a seven-night grid on which he was constantly placing and replacing his magnetic show cards.

Occasionally, he would whip around and bark a question to Bill Reubens, something about the compatibility between two shows, or the demographic appeal of one of the competition's formidable fixtures on a certain night.

Bill was barely visible behind a mound of seven loose-leaf

notebooks that were brimming with some kind of data. No matter what the question, Bill would inevitably have to leave the room for the answer. What was in those books anyway—figures for the next day's races at Belmont?

About three in the afternoon this ritual was interrupted by the company butler, who walked up to Silverman with a silver platter, on top of which sat a simple white note folded in half.

Silverman looked at the note, then passed it to Bob Mulholland. After Bob perused it, Fred turned to him and said, "Tell News that we'll preempt Disney tonight, and they can go seven o'clock to eight o'clock. If they need more time, they can also have eleven-thirty, after the late news."

The solemnity of Fred's tone had us all concerned. Irwin Segelstein, being the ranking elder statesman and Fred's closest friend at NBC, occupied the head seat at the opposite end of the table. It was he who broke the silence.

"What's going on, Fred? Did something happen?"

Fred, already distracted by the magnetic cards, looked up and said, "Uh, the Pope died."

When Irwin heard this, he rose from his chair, began pacing back and forth, wringing his hands, and muttering over and over again, "This is terrible. Just terrible. What are we going to do? What are we going to do?"

Fred was getting irritated. "Irwin, I told you what we're going to do. News'll preempt Disney, and then go again at eleven-thirty if they need to."

"I know that," said Irwin. "But what about after that? I just can't believe this is happening to us."

"Us?" exclaimed Fred. "What are you talking about, Irwin? The Pope died. You're Jewish."

Irwin stopped in his tracks.

"Oh, the *Pope* died. I thought you said *Hope* died."

There are some great TV people whom you don't have to look for. They just seem to materialize one day at center stage and take it from there. Eddie Murphy was like that. When I first saw Eddie, he was brand-new to the cast of *Saturday Night Live,* one of a half-dozen actors seated around a table and reading through a script. He was about twenty and totally innocent of the big time; he was, for all practical purposes, still an extra. But whenever he opened his mouth, he was getting huge laughs; the entire staff had stopped what they were doing and were marveling at his extraordinary *presence.* It was as if his words had been put through some kind of voice enhancer. "Where'd *he* come from?" everyone was asking one another. "Who *is* this guy?"

Three years later, I actually got to appear with Eddie, by then a certified star, on *Saturday Night Live.* Let me be frank—I'm a ham. There are some people in the Hollywood television community who think I'll do anything to perform—even mall openings. So when Dick Ebersol asked me if I'd like to do *Saturday Night Live,* I didn't need much in the way of encouragement. Unfortunately, the experience taught me something about the real world of acting. What it taught me was that acting is like stock-car racing: It may look like fun, but you really don't want to get out there with the pros.

On the afternoon of the broadcast, I impressed myself by not being in the least bit nervous. What was my secret? Ignorance. Until I actually did it I had no idea what it would be like to stand in front of 10 million people on live TV and perform material that was being written and rewritten right up to airtime. It wasn't until the dress rehearsal that I started to lose my composure.

The *SNL* dress rehearsal takes place before a studio audience at seven-thirty on the night of the show. Eddie Murphy and I were in a sketch together, both playing ourselves. The basic premise was that I was trying to get him to defect from *Saturday Night Live* and accept his own series on NBC. The dialogue needed work, though, so as we waited in the wings for another sketch to be blocked out, Eddie and I were writing lines, with occasional help from Joe Piscopo or one of the other regulars who would wander by. By the time we were sent to perform for the dress-rehearsal audience, I thought we'd improved the script a lot.

What I didn't know was that Eddie was going to improve it even more.

Everything was fine until I got to a line that said, "Eddie, if you leave *Saturday Night Live* and come with me, I'll make you bigger than Gary Coleman."

At that point, Eddie took it upon himself to ad-lib: "Hey, my *dick* is bigger than Gary Coleman."

Exit Eddie.

Enter panic.

So what did I do? I stood there like a dope for a full forty-five seconds while the audience's laughter rolled over me like a tidal wave—and when you're onstage, a forty-five-second laugh is an eternity.

And it will be another eternity before I ever get back in the comedy ring with Eddie Murphy.

NINE

A Sitcom Named Desire

T elevision didn't achieve ad-
olescence until it was more than thirty years old—but then
the medium made up for lost time. The 1980s saw the flour-
ishing of cable, VCRs, the Fox Network, and MTV. Besides
that, every one of the three original networks changed hands.
Capital Cities Corporation bought ABC; Laurence Tisch
took over CBS; and GE acquired NBC. In essence, smart,
shrewd businessmen entered the fray just when the mature
business of network television needed them most. But only
Cap Cities came with a strong broadcast background and
expertise. Ken Auletta has written a book called *Three Blind
Mice* that discusses the ramifications of all these develop-

ments in intricate detail. Ultimately, though, it's a rather simple story: Everything changed—except the most basic thing. For all the technological advances, for all the management upheaval, television, at bottom, is still what it always was: *a business of ideas.*

In some ways this makes television a very simple game. When you have good, workable ideas, and when you know what to do with them, you succeed. Ideas are the key to everything. If you have a good idea for a show, you can interest a talented producer. The producer, in turn, will hire a top writer. As a result, you have a quality script. A quality script will attract a topflight actor, and a topflight actor will attract an audience.

Of course, that's *if* you have a good idea. This is where things can get complicated—and where, as GE and Laurence Tisch found, television bears little resemblance to the consumer electronics or hotel businesses.

Good ideas don't come along very often and they can't be constructed at will. I myself have had at least one *Misfits of Science* and one *Manimal* for every *Miami Vice.* That's to be expected, and it's nothing to get depressed about. It takes just a few good creative flashes to work economic wonders.

Consider our platinum Thursday—which was sparked by the freshness and originality of Bill Cosby's monologues on *The Tonight Show* and elsewhere. Those monologues, honed over twenty-five years, served as the basis for 175 great half hours of television. All Cosby needed was someone to notice he was working with some great ideas.

Cosby eventually became the cornerstone for an evening that appealed strongly to eighteen-to-forty-nine-year-olds, a demographic group that movie studios will pay a hefty premium to reach, especially on a night when many people are making plans for the weekend. (The night drew a lot of retail advertisements as well, but movie advertising was a key reason Thursday evening generated a phenomenal $250 million a year in revenues for NBC in the late eighties.)

Naturally, I was delighted that things turned out that way. But was I thinking of demographics or Hollywood studio ad budgets when we were arranging that fearsome foursome of comedies: *Cosby, Family Ties, Cheers,* and *Night Court?* No. All I knew was what Lee Currlin, master programmer at NBC, had taught me: the most effective way to counterprogram an aging character show like *Magnum, P.I.,* for example, was by crossing the form—going with a younger-appeal comedy. Four great production teams outdid themselves each week in making America laugh. And as a result, NBC got to laugh all the way to the bank.

But you can't start with a desire for obscene amounts of money and "inspire" anything except frustration. Sure, you can always develop demographically "correct" characters, but that gets you no closer to a watchable show than a Venus color-by-numbers painting gets to hanging in the Louvre. Arriving at a good idea is a messy, imperfect, hit-or-miss process. Here's how it happens in real life:

It's a rainy Saturday afternoon, and I am watching television with my seven-year-old niece, Carrie. We have two hours to kill before my wife comes back from running errands and we can go to dinner, and we are zapping through the channels, trying to find something we can mutually tolerate. Ours is a battle not of wits, but of short attention spans, until we land on the old movie *How to Marry a Millionaire* with Marilyn Monroe, Betty Grable, and Lauren Bacall. I put my mind on automatic pilot and settle back.

Somehow, though, when Monday morning rolls around, I'm still thinking about *How to Marry a Millionaire.* "In the back of my television mind, I know there used to be a series by that name," I tell my staff. "I don't know if we'd need to buy the rights, but a bunch of women living in an apartment and looking for Mr. Right—like the *Apartment 3-G* comic strip—maybe that's something we should consider. Let's get some women writers in here, and we'll discuss it."

The first writer found the idea repulsive. "How can you suggest in this day and age that a woman needs to be married—and to a wealthy man?" she said.

The second writer used the word "disgusting."

The third writer said she wouldn't take money from people who thought up such a sexist concept.

By the time writer number four stormed out, I was pretty sure this wasn't going to be one of our blue-chip ideas, let alone a project destined for the Museum of Broadcasting.

Flash forward to our regional affiliate meeting in Miami, not far from where my father's sister lived. The only time I had available to visit Aunt Lil was on Sunday morning before the meetings started, so she invited me for breakfast. We were soon joined by Fritzy, her friend from across the hall. Fritzy asked Aunt Lil to fix her a bagel, then complained as soon as it was served. "You always burn the bagel. Don't you know with my teeth I can't eat bagels that are this brown?" Lil then fixed her with a stare and said, "Well, at least I still have eyes good enough to get a driver's license. Without me, who would drive you to Pumpernicks for the Early Bird Special?" I sat there watching this and thought, This is like *How to Marry a Millionaire*—minus the sexism. When you're in your twenties or thirties or even your forties, it *is* repulsive and depressing to think that marrying a successful man is the solution to your life. But if you have a mother or aunt who's sixty years old and living alone, then you'd probably be thrilled to hear that she'd linked up with a doctor or some well-to-do widower.

I thought maybe I was onto something—but then, I'd thought that before. My problem was finding a woman writer to discuss the idea with, one who would stay in the room long enough for us to get through the entire pitch. Unfortunately, we'd already alienated most of the better female comedy talents in town. Then Warren Littlefield, at that time vice president in charge of comedy, spoke up and said, "Why don't we try Susan Harris?" That was a brilliant suggestion, but Susan Harris was a tough get. She was—and is—a superb writer of TV comedy who happened to be a woman. Harris's work had regularly addressed the kind of social issues that had previously been the exclusive domain of talk shows. To sign her up for this new project—which we were alternately calling *How to Marry a Millionaire for Women Over Fifty* or *Miami Nice* for short—would have been a major coup. She and her partners, husband Paul Junger Witt and Tony Thomas, had several hit comedy series, including *Soap* and *Benson*. But Harris had been telling people that she was burned out on sitcoms and, though only in her late thirties, eager to retire. So I was somewhat surprised that she even agreed to come in and listen to our pitch. I was thrilled when she paused a beat, looked back at the drooling executives

....

gathered at her feet, and said, "I'll write that show for free."

The Golden Girls came together from the start like an idea that was meant to be. Because, as I've noted earlier, there aren't many roles written for mature women, we had about four great choices for every one of the leading parts. The only casting complication came with Bea Arthur, who was off doing a play in New York and wasn't originally among the candidates. Bea didn't sign on until Lee Grant decided that she didn't want to play someone old enough to have grand-children and dropped out of the running. The show itself changed very little from the way it was originally conceived. The only modification made after the pilot was that Susan Harris decided to drop a gay male character who lived with the four older women as a sort of housekeeper and confidant. It wasn't the character's sexuality that troubled her, but something else. "I don't like what that character implies," she said after the initial taping. "These women can take care of themselves."

She was certainly right about that—as any of the directors who tried to get too bossy with Bea Arthur, Estelle Getty, Rue McClanahan, or Betty White can testify. Those women knew what they were doing on a soundstage, and while they were always professional and got along very well with each other, they didn't suffer fools gladly. Probably a half-dozen "A" directors marched boldly onto *The Golden Girls* set that first year; most found themselves chewed up and spit back out.

On paper, *The Golden Girls* was a show that didn't look good. And for the most obvious reason: It was about people with gray hair. The summer before it came on, the advertising agencies who handicap each TV season predicted it would get a 23 share. None of that bothered me, because I'd seen the pilot and thought it was one of the most hysterical half hours I'd ever seen. If people sampled the show, they'd be hooked, so we premiered it two weeks before the official opening of the season, on a night when NBC was carrying the Miss America Pageant and viewership would be especially high.

The Golden Girls opened with a 45 share, and we never looked back. Since we'd decided to put the show on Saturday—a night where we'd been whipped so badly in the prime-time ratings the TV critics took to calling our lineup "Saturday Night Dead"—that success was especially important to us, and everyone in the industry knew it. Harvey Shephard—the head programmer at CBS, then the number-one network—sent me a gracious letter the following Monday that said, "Congratulations on winning the season." All this before the starting gun for the 1985–86 season had been fired.

The hit shows in television are often the ones that defy logic and break the rules. Or to quote conventional TV wisdom more precisely: "The hits are the flukes." Interestingly enough, audience research told us that *The Golden Girls* wasn't a show that appealed only to an older audience. Very young children liked the noise and commotion the women made when they argued. Teenagers fixated on the Estelle Getty character, who, because of a stroke, had lost the controlling mechanism we all have that keeps us from saying whatever pops into our minds. Her character dispensed with all the social conventions. A little old lady calling people "slob" and "slut" appealed to kids immensely. But the key reason for the *The Golden Girls*'s success is that it had what I call a S.U.P., or Satisfying Underlying Premise.

Big hits usually have an S.U.P., a secret ingredient that makes people feel good about their lives besides just entertaining or informing them. There is something in the basic premise of the show that validates some reassuring notion the audience would like to believe is real. Take *Northern Exposure,* for example. Most people in America live in big cities. These urban Americans are wont to fantasize that they can someday live in a small town, a place where people don't have to lock their doors at night, and where they know their neighbors. Most people will never realize that fantasy. But if they want to visit it and have it reinforced, they need only travel to CBS Monday nights at 10:00. With a show like *Dallas* or *Dynasty* the S.U.P. is that most people are poor, not rich, and never will be rich. But they can take solace that their problems pale in comparison to the problems of the characters in those serials.

What about a news show like *60 Minutes?* Most of us spend our lives feeling taken advantage of by big institutions and/or big business. We'd like to believe there is a force out there exposing the corruption of the Big Boys. The S.U.P. at *60 Minutes* is that here is a band of crusaders who ferret out the truth on our behalf.

Finally, *The Golden Girls* addressed a profound fear—the fear of finding yourself alone and unhappy in your later years. The message—the S.U.P.—of *The Golden Girls* was that old age and unpleasant times are not synonymous if you have good friends and a positive attitude.

· · ·

Good ideas don't just *make* money. They can also keep you from committing billion-dollar fiascoes.

I am speaking literally here.

One morning in 1989, I got a call at home from my boss, Bob Wright. It was 6:30 A.M. L.A. time, so the minute I heard Bob's voice, I knew something was very wrong.

"I've got bad news about this baseball negotiation we're involved in," he said. Then he explained that he had just bid $780 million for the network rights to the major league baseball-game package over the next four years. NBC was prepared to go as high as $870 million; at that price, Bob said, the network could still break even on the broadcasts. But what worried him was that Peter Ueberroth, then the baseball commissioner, had just called to intimate that if NBC wasn't prepared to go up to at least $1 billion—the amount CBS (which never had baseball) was set to offer—then he shouldn't even bother raising his bid.

"Brandon," Bob said, "I know how much you love baseball. I'm aware of the numbers it gets. But I don't think we can responsibly bid that kind of money."

This *was* a very tough call. Every network would like to provide its affiliates with events that are glamorous, prestigious, and sure ratings-getters. Events like the World Series and All-Star games. These programs are unique, so when your network carries them, the viewer has to come to you. And keeping the affiliates happy is the national pastime for networks.

So, even though the numbers had reached ludicrous levels, we knew why CBS was still in the bidding. Their prime-time lineup was so weak at that point that the CBS affiliates had good reason to jump ship; for Larry Tisch's people, acquiring the baseball rights was a desperate stop-gap measure to hold the line against mass defections and affiliate dissatisfaction. If CBS owned these rights, they could say to their affiliates in Tulsa, Bangor, or Cleveland, "Hey, you can leave us if you want, but for the next four years you're not going to have the World Series, the play-offs, or the All-Star game. In fact, if you leave us, you're going to have to compete with those programs. So good luck."

NBC was in a different—and much stronger—position. We were the leaders in prime time. And we had already been the network of major league baseball for forty-three years. Still, with a $1-billion-plus price tag, even if we sold every second of commercial time at a premium rate, we estimated we would lose about $100 million a year or more. As much as we, too, wanted to keep our affiliates content, you had to wonder if staying in the bidding really made sense.

In addition, it galled me to think that the $500 million profit we'd made in prime time the year before was not only going to pay the escalating salaries of superstars, but would also make millionaires out of shortstops who hit .227 and pitchers coming off of 6–10 seasons.

"It's going to kill me not to be able to sit in the commissioner's box at the World Series," I told Bob. "But this contract isn't worth what you've already offered, never mind what they're asking for. Give me ten or twenty million extra for our prime-time budget, and we'll find a way to compete with baseball."

That idea was appealing to me because no one had ever

really "competed" against baseball before. Under the old system of divvying up the games, which changed with this contract, the package was split between two networks, who would take turns broadcasting the league play-offs and the World Series in alternate years. Thus, if you were the network carrying the Series, you didn't want to compete too hard against the play-offs, which, after all, were building interest for the event you were preparing to show. Likewise, if the other guys had the Series and you had the play-offs, you didn't want to hurt an event that you'd be carrying the following year—and which you'd be selling to advertisers based on the ratings your competitor achieved. Now, though, the rules had been changed—and I was ready to roll up my sleeves.

With his blessing—and deep pockets—I went to work.

In thinking about how to program against the World Series, I asked myself, Who is the audience that doesn't want to watch baseball? Since we were living in an age when there was more than one TV set in many households, it made sense to identify, and then try to target, the nonfan.

Again, an image of a single individual came to mind. Or actually, it was a married individual—my wife, Lilly. I love my wife, and I love baseball, but they are mutually exclusive. She could care less who was playing whom, unless the Dodgers were in the game and the series had gone to game six or seven. While not every woman had Lilly's indifference to the sport, I bet there were a lot of Lillys out there. I bet $20 million, in fact. A lot of money, until you compared it to what CBS was spending during this comparable period.

Fade out/fade in: to a press conference at what is now the Universal Hilton in Universal City. I am announcing NBC's antibaseball strategy while standing before huge color por-traits of Jackie Collins and Danielle Steel. Working with Tony Masucci, the head of NBC movies and miniseries, we directed NBC productions—our in-house movie studio—to produce one miniseries based on Collins's best-seller *Lucky* and to tie up the rights to twenty-nine Danielle Steel novels, many of which were mega-best-sellers. Rather than competing with the World Series, we were betting that a Jackie Collins mini-series and two back-to-back Danielle Steel made-for-TV mov-ies would be a powerful enough triple-header to be an alternative to it. Let the Oakland A's and the Cincinnati Reds get their hits, we figured. We'd get ours.

The strategy worked better than I expected, largely be-cause, as usual, I hadn't been thinking in terms of all the economic possibilities—just the audience and the shows. Not only did those miniseries draw huge numbers of female view-ers who didn't care about baseball; they provided a windfall in terms of sales to overseas markets, where Danielle Steel and Jackie Collins were best-selling authors in over thirty lan-guages, and their miniseries became equally hot commodi-ties. Based on that success, in fact, we commissioned Steel to write a bible for a one-hour dramatic series that NBC Produc-tions would sell to European markets with her name above the title. She wound up doing such an extraordinary job that the bible was published in the United States in May 1992 as a novel called *Jewels*. Like everything she writes, it became an instant best-seller.

I have seen some weird and wonderful things happen when people sit down to discuss TV ideas. I have seen, for example,

one bad and one half-baked idea come together and create
an idea so good that it ratcheted a whole network up several
notches.

The time, winter of 1980; the place, La Scala Restaurant in
Beverly Hills. On one side of the lunch table sits the NBC
contingent: myself and Michael Zinberg, our vice president
of comedy development. Both of us are there to convey the
vision of our boss, Fred Silverman, who at that moment is
likely lamenting how NBC has become snakebit since he
signed on.

About ten years before he came to the network, Fred had
forged a reputation as a boy wonder at CBS. While still in his
early thirties he'd presided over such important shows as
Mary Tyler Moore, M*A*S*H, and *All in the Family.* Then he'd
moved over to ABC, where he'd worked a new and very different set of wonders with shows like *The Love Boat, Three's
Company, Laverne & Shirley, Charlie's Angels,* and *Roots.* With
Fred at the helm, both of those networks had become number one in the ratings. But at NBC very little had gone right
for him, and failure hung over him like a fog. Fred's style in
those days was to scream a lot, pound his fist on his desk—
and constantly take his programming off in different direc-
tions.

Not everything he did at NBC, it should be pointed out,
was a disaster. Fred was responsible, in 1979, for *Real People,*
a show that launched the trend toward "reality" television
that, as I write this, is the most widespread it's ever been.
Network shows like *Unsolved Mysteries, America's Most Wanted,*
and *Cops* are examples, as are syndicated offerings like *Hard
Copy* and *A Current Affair.* And Fred got NBC back into the

comedy game again with series such as *Diff'rent Strokes,* which ran eight years, and *The Facts of Life,* which ran nine. Still, in truth, the bad news far outweighed the good. And as things got worse, Fred began to lose confidence not in his own judgment, but in others' ability to execute his programming ideas. He careened from serious, service-oriented shows like *Lifeline* to campy fare like *Buck Rogers* to expensive tries like *Supertrain* to the aforementioned *Pink Lady.*

As it happened, at the time of the lunch at La Scala, Fred was on one of his "quality" kicks. Which was fine. But it was hard to tell exactly what Fred meant by that. Fred wasn't dumb by any means; he had extraordinary street smarts as well as a master's degree in broadcasting from Ohio State. It's just that he worked mostly by instinct.

In a one-on-one pitch session with Fred I once suggested that we might consider doing a comedy series patterned after *A Streetcar Named Desire.*

"Yeah?" Fred said. "Brando was in the movie. Yeah. So what?"

"Well, yes," I said. "But it was a play before that. You know, Tennessee Williams? It's the story of this guy Stanley Kowalski and the tension that surfaces when his sister-in-law, Blanche DuBois, comes to visit him and his wife. They really go at each other—kind of like Archie and Meathead."

"Really?" Fred said. "So why doesn't Stanley just tell Blanche to get the fuck out?"

"Gee, Fred, I don't know," I said. "Tennessee Williams never really raises that possibility, so . . ."

"Well, listen," Fred said. "Unless you can tell me why he

doesn't throw her ass out of the house, you don't have a goddamn show."

Back to La Scala.

Zinberg and I were lunching that day with Steven Bochco and Michael Kozoll, then working as a team for Grant Tinker's production company, MTM. The two producers were a study in contrasting styles. Bochco is dark, suave, handsome, and an excellent raconteur. Kozoll is reserved, dour, and rumpled. Kozoll's the kind of guy who'll walk up to you, shake your hand, and say, "Hey, haven't you put on some weight? You gotta watch that." Not an easy person to deal with.

At that point, Bochco and Kozoll were not exactly major players in the entertainment business. At NBC Bochco had produced a short-lived sitcom called *Turnabout* and he and another MTM producer, Bruce Paltrow, had done an hour-long doctor show for us called *Operating Room* that never got past the pilot stage. He'd also gone nowhere at CBS and ABC with shows called, respectively, *Paris* and *Vampire*. Kozoll had respectable writing credits, but even fewer development credentials than Steven. They seemed to work well together. I liked Steven. Even when he failed, his failures were always interesting. He explored characters in a depth not usually seen on TV. He had a great ear for dialogue and a great eye for the absurd. He took risks.

Bochco and Kozoll got the ball rolling by pitching an anthology show set in a San Francisco hotel. It would have an ensemble cast, they said, and be part comedy but mostly drama. Michael and I had problems with the idea. A hotel, we pointed out, is not an inherently dramatic setting. Nothing *has* to happen there; nothing *must* be resolved. I saw them facing an uphill battle every week, weaving the hotel into the plot while trying to create situations that would hold the viewers' interest. (Little did I know that a few years later Aaron Spelling would actually transform Arthur Hailey's *Hotel* into a *Love Boat*–type anthology and have a whopping five-year hit.)

Now it was our turn. We had come to lunch ready to pitch *them* an idea—an idea that Fred and I had discussed, and that he kept referring to as "*Barney Miller* outdoors." This would be a show about policemen, we told them, a drama that examined the cops' private and professional lives. The idea was, in truth, basically the same one that we'd tried with *Operating Room* but that didn't work. We determined from audience research that people didn't like hearing about doctors' drinking problems, girlfriend troubles, and assorted character flaws. Besides, when people go to a hospital they are petrified with fear. They're sick and all they want to do is get well. They'd prefer *not* to know that their surgeon was in a hot tub with a flight attendant until three in the morning. "I think the audience will be more forgiving of cops," Zinberg told Bochco and Kozoll. "Policemen are blue-collar workers. They're regular people, not instruments of God. Their other big plus is that they work in police stations, in squad cars, and on streets, any one of which has a setting with more potential jeopardy than an examining room or, for that matter, a hotel lobby." The show we were proposing would be set in the worst police precinct in the worst kind of crime-ridden city neighborhood. A real war zone. Each week we would watch our warriors do battle and later try to decompress.

Bochco spoke up first. "I don't want to do a cop show," he said. "We just did a solid one, *Paris,* with James Earl Jones, and we couldn't get arrested—all puns intended. I'm sick of them. *Everybody* is sick of them. Cop shows," he said, "are the old TV."

"Well, there are no cop shows in the top twenty right now, and that could mean one of two things," I said. "It could mean that no one wants to watch these kinds of shows anymore. Or it could mean that we've spotted an opportunity, a need, and that people are ready to take a fresh look at the genre—if the show is done right."

So we struck a deal. A very simple deal. Bochco and Kozoll would do the show *we* wanted. But they got to do it the way *they* wanted. They would have almost complete freedom from network meddling: They could cast whomever they wanted, hire the quirky director Bob Butler, and put the scripts right into production without waiting for our notes or approval. I suppose I could have been insulted by their terms, but I wasn't. In the first place, I knew Bochco well enough to understand that this was his way of sticking it to the networks for meddling with, then ultimately bouncing, his last several shows. Besides that, I was overseeing about forty pilots, so if they had complete autonomy on their show, that was one less thing I had to worry about.

The rest, as they say, is history. *Hill Street Blues* turned out to be radically different from the rest of network television. The first time I realized this was when I wandered into the screening room at NBC where several NBC executives were watching the dailies of the pilot for the show—and having a meltdown. The raw footage of the morning roll-call scene that would become a trademark of *Hill Street* was making them crazy. Traditionally, when a scene is set in a large space like a police station house, the director and cinematographer take care to include a master shot, known as coverage, which shows the total area of the set. But what Bob Butler had done was to shoot the entire roll-call segment with a single hand-held camera. No coverage, no medium shots, no close-ups. "Where's the coverage?!" the executives were screaming in the darkness. "Where's the goddamn coverage?!"

The show was unconventional in many other ways, too. By the standards of textbook TV, *Hill Street* had way too many characters and subplots. You never knew who might get shot and die, or whether the episode you were watching would have a happy ending or a sad one. Nor did *Hill Street* unfold with familiar TV rhythms. In most crime shows, the so-called pitfalls come at the act-breaks that occur every eight minutes. Usually at these act-breaks either a car is going to come screeching down an alley, a body's going to fall out of a closet, or a character is going to pick up a phone and say, "Our leading suspect just turned up in the river." *Hill Street,* however, dispensed with these. The scripts were densely written but amorphous in shape. A typical episode would start in the station house and then move to Hill and Renko's squad car, then cut back to Furillo's office, and that in turn would lead to a scene in Davenport's bed. Each episode was "a day in the life," structured around a twenty-four-hour time clock. The show moved to the irregular beat of real life, and that could be confusing—at least in the beginning, before people got used to it.

And this was one show that *would* take some getting used to. The testing, in fact, produced some of the worst numbers Fred or I had ever seen. To his credit, though, Fred never wavered in his loyalty to the show. The fact that this *was* the quality program he'd been looking for buoyed him up, made him feel that maybe the good ship Peacock could be turned around. "This is something completely different," he said. "And completely different always tests badly."

We were so proud of the *Hill Street* pilot that we decided to present it to our "A" list of advertisers and our affiliate representatives in a special way. Usually, we produced a ten-minute clip of a new show and screened it for those folks as part of a three-hour presentation that included a glimpse of our entire fall lineup. This time we rented the Guild Theater on Fiftieth Street in Manhattan and ran the whole episode. It ended with Officers Hill and Renko, two characters whom we had come to know and root for, being gunned down in a random shoot-out.

When the lights came on, the audience was stunned, both by the sudden, violent turn of the plot, and by the overall power of what they'd just witnessed. I had seen this scene several times in screenings, and every time it got to me. This day was no different. Still feeling the impact of the show, I walked up to the stage. It was time to introduce Daniel Travanti, who'd played Captain Frank Furillo. You could feel the admiration for him in the room. The audience gave him a huge ovation. Every eye in the house was trained on him, every ear waited for him to speak.

Let me pause here to say that in all my years in the entertainment business, I've never gotten close to any actors, and
this story always reminds me of why. "Ladies and gentlemen,"
I said. "I am truly honored to introduce . . . Daniel Travanti."
Travanti stood at center stage waiting for a few moments,
basking in all the glory. Then he spoke.

"It's Tra-*van*ti, Brandon. Not Tra-*vaun*ti."

It doesn't matter how big the moment; an actor's ego is
always bigger.

Usually, when we screen pilots, it's the affiliates who nitpick
and bust chops. A week later at the Century Plaza in L.A.,
though, the affiliates were unanimous in their support. One
of them, in fact, should take credit for saving two of the
show's more popular characters. "I know this is art and all
that," said Bruce McGorrill, an avuncular Yankee type who
was the general manager of the NBC affiliate in Portland,
Maine. "But you shouldn't kill off two of your best lead
characters in the first episode. They were great together, and
you could spin them off later." I passed along his comment
to Bochco and Kozoll, who went along with the idea of letting
Hill and Renko live. It was easy enough to accomplish. All
they had to do was reshoot the final scene: Instead of Furillo
picking up the phone and saying, "One DOA, one critical,"
he instead says, "They're both in intensive care."

So was the show, for quite a while. *Hill Street Blues* played
on Saturday nights at 10:00 P.M. against the ABC juggernaut
Fantasy Island. The numbers were abysmal. *Hill Street* got a 19
share at a time when a 27 share was the dividing line between
renewal and cancellation. The next week it dropped even
further. Hearing these overnights every Sunday morning was

bad enough. But listening to poor Nancy Mead's quivering voice when she called to deliver the news was awful. What Nancy didn't know when she took the job was that Fred Silverman occasionally had a kill-the-messenger mentality. Since my name came right after Fred's alphabetically, she'd still be shaken, when she reached me, from the way Fred had yelled at *her* about *Hill Street*'s lousy ratings.

From the moment the first episode aired, though, the critics were on our side—and that probably was one reason why Fred never wavered in his support of the show. Their raves for *Hill Street* were universal, and since there weren't many things they could write bouquets about at NBC, *Hill Street* wasn't taken for granted. I'd felt like the Elephant Man until *Hill Street*. Everywhere I went, people had to struggle to find something nice to say to me. "Oh, you work at NBC," they'd say. "It must be, uh, nice to work in television." Now what I was hearing was, "Oh, yeah—you work at the network of *Hill Street Blues*."

I was a fan of the show myself. I identified with Furillo, the guy who was trying to keep his staff calm and orderly, who wanted to stop the forces on high from destroying the fragile equilibrium of his station. Fred watched it at home, too. One Monday he came in and said, "You know, Brandon, I turned on *Hill Street,* and I don't see how we can do any better than that. What do we have to do to get that rating up?" I suggested that maybe Saturday was the wrong night for such a realistic and sometimes even downbeat show. "Maybe it reminds people of why they're sitting home—they're afraid to go out," I said. "Maybe it would do better on a weeknight." Fred at first resisted: "You find me one piece of research to back that up," he said. But eventually he moved the show around until it finally settled on Thursdays at 10:00 P.M. The Nielsen number rose, but not by much. The show had only a 19 share when we renewed it for another season. (A year or so before, we had *canceled The Eddie Capra Mysteries,* a show that had a 31 share.) I later found out that at the time *Hill Street* was the lowest-rated show in network history ever to be renewed.

Why did we renew it? Two reasons. The first had to do with a piece of rather obscure research that somebody came up with when we were searching for a way to explain to the affiliates why we were behind the show. What this research said was that *Hill Street* was getting a higher rating in homes that had pay cable than in homes that didn't. That meant that the people who had the most options, the people who could choose from what was then about a twenty-channel cable universe, were seeking out our show to watch. To me that meant *Hill Street* was the kind of show networks would need to compete in the future, when cable would mean access to 50, 100, or even 150 channels. Today, shows like *Murphy Brown, Seinfeld,* and *Law and Order*—all of which gathered steam after initially low ratings—are examples of this trend. News programs such as *48 Hours* and *Primetime Live* fall into this category as well. After the results of *Hill Street,* we would renew several poorly rated new shows—including *St. Else- where, Family Ties,* and *Remington Steele*—strictly on the basis of their strength in key demographics and their pull in these cable-ready households.

There is, however, another important consideration here: Despite volumes of research, renewal decisions ultimately come down to instinct. As Kenny Rogers sings in "The Gambler," "You gotta know when to hold 'em, know when to fold 'em . . ." So in keeping with the gambling spirit, we renewed *Hill Street* simply because we liked it—at first simply for what it was, and then, as time went on, for the tremendous things it was doing for us as a network. *Hill Street* ran for seven seasons, and won twenty-six Emmys, the most ever for a dramatic series. By its third season, it was getting a 35 share and delivering a huge audience to the affiliates' eleven o'clock news broadcasts—which, by the way, is where local stations generate about 25 percent of their revenue. *Hill Street* taught us that patience pays off, even in the fast-paced world of network TV. And perhaps most important of all, it sent a message to the creative community, telling writers, producers, and directors that NBC was capable both of providing ideas and also of backing off and allowing for a measure of artistic freedom.

Oh, yes, there was one more thing: The television critics would, quite simply, have had us for a barbecue if we took the show off the air.

Hill Street may have also been the most fertile show in the history of TV, spawning more smash-hit—albeit surreptitious—spin-offs than anything before or since. After *Hill Street* had been on the air for a year, we had our research department do what's known as a maintenance study to determine what the audience was liking best and least about the stories and the characters in them. Somewhat to our surprise, it turned out that viewers wanted to see more of Belker, Howard Hunter, Renko, and other characters who were slightly around the bend. "Maybe we should try a show with *just* oddball characters," I said one day to Jeff Sagansky, who then looked at me like I could have definitely belonged in that show. Nevertheless, that notion was then combined with the sensibility and spirit of *The Road Warrior,* a big action movie that was released that summer, and eventually became the genesis for *The A-Team.*

The potency of *Hill Street* didn't end there. Affiliate Bruce McGorrill's notion of spinning off the black-and-white cop team of Hill and Renko was intriguing, so we brought the idea to MTM, the production company behind *Hill Street.* Even though MTM had a long history of doing spin-offs (*The Mary Tyler Moore Show,* after all, begat *Rhoda, Phyllis,* and *Lou Grant*), Arthur Price, head of MTM at the time, was reluctant to go ahead. He was nervous, he said, about upsetting the equilibrium of the *Hill Street* cast by removing a couple of key actors from the mix. His reluctance continued even after he was offered a fairly lucrative commitment for thirteen episodes of the new show. Finally, when Tony Yerkovich left MTM and struck out on his own, we brought the idea to him, and the show that eventually emerged from the discussion was *Miami Vice,* which was many things, but at its core, it had a Southern white cop and his black partner just like you-know-who from you-know-where.

Yet another show to come out of *Hill Street* was *St. Elsewhere.* *St. Elsewhere* was our second and much more successful attempt to execute *Operating Room,* a pilot that, as I mentioned earlier, was actually the predecessor to *Hill Street.* When Bruce Paltrow, the producer, saw our classy variation on the traditional cop show, he got the message that NBC was committed to being less conventional than your average TV network. That led him to construct a first cousin to that idea—*St. Elsewhere*. As it happened, two budding behind-the-scenes stars—Joshua Brand and John Falsey—had just finished doing eight weeks of intensive research at a big-city hospital to develop story lines for a show they hoped to produce. Brand and Falsey, who have since gone on to produce *A Year in the Life, Northern Exposure,* and *I'll Fly Away,* teamed up with Paltrow and created an astounding dramatic series that ran for six solid seasons.

But one can't list the "Sons of *Hill Street*" without mentioning *L.A. Law.* That show came out of a very brief meeting with Steven Bochco in 1985—and it proves that simple ideas are often the most powerful ones. "*Hill Street* is about eighty-five percent cops and fifteen percent lawyers," I said. "Why don't we flip the proportions and see what happens?" What happens is a show that was a far bigger hit from the get-go than *Hill Street,* and almost its equal in Emmy attention. It's now going into its seventh season, a longevity *Hill Street* also achieved. All of which suggests that like good racehorses, thoroughbred ideas (when they're well executed) breed strong and true.

One thing I've always loved about the TV business is dealing directly with the idea people. I even loved having certain people tell me if an idea I happened to have stunk up the joint—no mean feat given the seductive lure of the tidy sums NBC might offer them to go off and turn one of those smelly notions into a series pilot. I loved listening to pitches, talking things over with producers or writers who came in with five eighths or two sevenths of an idea. That was me and Gary

David Goldberg going mano a mano at a table at the old
Ships Restaurant on Wilshire Boulevard, thrashing out what
show Gary would agree to do for us at NBC. Ships, for those
not familiar with L.A.'s more affordable dining experiences,
is basically a diner with a gimmick: Every table has its own
toaster. I desperately wanted to get Gary away from CBS to do
a smart half-hour comedy for us. Gary wanted to interest me
in a script that had just been rejected by CBS. Usually I don't
cotton to cast-offs, but I picked up on the fact that *Family Ties*
was not just a show Gary was pitching. This was his life—an
ex-hippie couple settling down to raise their conservative
kids. The clash could work. But an hour?

A lot depended on those brainstorming sessions: Five years
before our meal at Ships, Gary had been living in a cave in
Greece, had bummed around San Diego for a while, and then
found his way to Hollywood. Now a respected producer looking to create his first hit, Gary was open to suggestions. I had
only one: redo his script (and the premise) as a half-hour
show.

A few years later, after *Family Ties* had established itself as
the second-most-popular show on NBC behind *Cosby*, Gary
would own two hundred acres in Vermont and a house in
Malibu. Quite a swing of fortune. And yet that day at Ships,
Gary, though only a would-be producer at that point, dealt
with me from a position of strength. He had, after all, a very
good idea. And, I guess, so did I. Because he said yes.

To stay on the air these days, a successful network television
show needs to attract about 15 to 20 million viewers each
week. Maybe in a perfect world TV would be something else.

But in the real world, TV is a populist medium, and so the challenge comes down to finding ideas that will capture the zeitgeist. I used to tell my staff at NBC that we all, at any moment, should be prepared to name two books on the best-seller list, two movies in the top five, and two records on the top ten. If we couldn't do that, then we weren't paying attention to the world around us—to what America was culturally investing in—and we were going to fail. I used to look very hard at TV commercials for ideas; more thought—and more money—goes into each frame of a commercial than even the most elaborate feature films. The producers Glen and Les Charles felt the same way I did about commercials. Back when we were trying to turn the network around, Fred Silverman, Michael Zinberg, and I recruited them away from ABC and *Taxi* to create a show for us. They came back with an idea for a comedy in the spirit of those Miller Lite beer commercials—with Rodney Dangerfield, John Madden, Yogi Berra (the inspiration for Coach), and a host of others—that were in fact among the funnier things on TV at that time. We said, Fine, go do it. As I write this, they still *are* doing it, eleven seasons later. But for about the first year of its prebroadcast life, *Cheers* was referred to at NBC as the "Miller Lite" show.

On the other hand, you could be a walking, talking what's-hot-and-what's-not list and still screw up badly.

In the late eighties, I thought I'd spotted a trend back toward more permissiveness, especially after films like *Blue Velvet* and *sex, lies and videotape* became cult favorites. At the same time Aaron Spelling, one of the most successful TV producers of all time, came in and pitched me a show about beautiful student nurses in Dallas. It would be set, he said, "in a hospital where the air-conditioning wasn't working properly, so their white cotton uniforms kind of cling." America's mores seem to swing like a pendulum every few years, so I persuaded myself that the country might be in the mood for just this kind of old-fashioned titillation.

I was wrong.

Nightingales got attacked by women's groups and written off by the critics as cheesy, soft-core porn, and we canceled it after thirteen episodes. The ratings were actually acceptable (21 share), but the mass advertiser boycotts were not. Once, at the height of the controversy, I went to visit my father-in-law in the hospital, and a nurse took me aside. "You better hope you're never sick," she said. "We know you did that show, and we'll be waiting."

A bad television show, I've always contended, is like America's involvement in Vietnam. Something that complicated and regrettable couldn't happen all at once. Someone would notice and say, "No way." Rather, when you create a true disaster, you start out with the best of intentions and the loftiest of purposes—and then things happen. To cope with those things, you start making a series of small, ill-advised compromises. And then one day you wake up—and you're in Vietnam. But before I tell you about the worst of all disasters, let me share some of the larger skirmishes along the way. The list that follows is one I've been known to refer to as NBC's "Decade of Excellence":

1980:   *Pink Lady* (what a concept: It was like Tony Orlando and Dawn—except Dawn didn't speak English).

1981:   *Lewis & Clark* (a sitcom that sent viewers on a channel-changing expedition).

1982:   *Gavilan* (James Bond for television; its share of the audience was 007).

1983:   *Manimal* (about a scientist who could transform himself into any species of animal; unfortunately, the show was stuck on "dog").

1984:   *Partners in Crime* (with Loni Anderson and Lynda Carter; best known around the network as "Terms of Endowment").

1985:   *Misfits of Science* (the world's tallest star—7-foot-4-inches—in one of the shortest-running series of all time).

1986:   *1986* (an aptly named NBC newsmagazine hosted by Roger Mudd; nobody ever had to worry about updating the title).

1987:   *The Highwayman* (about a high-tech eighteen-wheeler; one series that definitely failed to keep on truckin').

1988:   *Nightingales* (or, as I like to think of it, "The One Time That Sex Didn't Sell").

1989:   *The Nutt House* (series creator Mel Brooks wanted to do something different; I wish he had stuck to comedy).

1990:   *Hull High* (a high school musical that even if your own kid was the star, you couldn't sit through it).

But the all-time classic Vietnam fiasco, the one that stands out like a beacon, is *Supertrain*. Here's how it began:

It was August of 1978. I was in a meeting with several NBC

executives when Fred Silverman turned to Paul Klein and said, "Why don't you tell Brandon your idea about the train?"

"Do you really want me to?" Klein said coyly.

"Yeah, yeah, tell him," Fred said. "It's a great idea."

That was the first time I heard about *Supertrain.*

Klein was already a legend in the business and at NBC. He was the man who invented the term "jiggle show" in the *Charlie's Angels* era; "Mr. High Concept," he called himself. His idea of a joke was to refer to me as "Random Tarti-koff"—and later "a figment of Grant Tinker's irresponsibil-ity." He used to say even worse things about Fred—until he came in one day and found that Fred was his boss. By '78, he sensed that his days at NBC were numbered unless he could come up with a big idea, the Show That Would Turn the Network Around. *Supertrain,* he felt, was just that show.

I have to admit he could pitch an idea with the best of them. "There's this train," he began that day, his voice full of intrigue. "And on this train, there's a swimming pool, a disco, there are exercise rooms, there's a ballroom, there are four-star restaurants. This train is so big that each of its wheels goes on an entire set of tracks! It's that huge! And it goes from New York to Los Angeles in thirty-six hours! And every week, there'll be a different story! There'll be comedy! There'll be drama! There'll be legendary guest stars!"

The idea did have one big problem, though: No indepen-dent producer who'd heard it wanted to proceed—especially when they heard the accelerated (read impossible) produc-tion schedule necessary to make a midseason air date. Fred was so anxious for what could be a "hit the ground running" hit he was pushing to have the show ready in about four months, or about half the standard production time. Even though there would be a considerable amount of money involved, they all said it couldn't be done; there were obstacles on every level, starting with the fact that it made no sense. Why would all sorts of wealthy and interesting people be on the Supertrain instead of a plane? And how could anyone expect brilliant scripts that mixed mystery and comedy every week on a normal TV-series deadline?

Any experienced producer would know that he stood a good chance of *losing* a career on a gamble like this.

"Do yourself a favor and forget about this," said Hollywood producer Eddie Milkis, who had worked on *Silver Streak,* a movie with Richard Pryor and Gene Wilder that had been set on a train. "We worked for three years on our film, and the story didn't hold up for the whole movie. You're trying to do an Alfred Hitchcock movie on a train every week and get it out by January. This is impossible."

Klein saw the show as vital to his career, though. And so he kept pitching it around until he found a willing and respected producer named Dan Curtis—who told him that *Supertrain* was a great idea, *if only he'd stop thinking so small.*

A few weeks later, Curtis and Klein called everyone into the conference room in Burbank, where they'd set up the most elaborate train set I've ever seen. This was the prototype for the Supertrain, and though it must have cost a fortune, its sole purpose was to impress the people in that room. The cars opened up to reveal intricate little rooms decorated with expensive dollhouse furniture. "This is going to be *The Love Boat* on rails," Curtis said. I couldn't help feeling cynical; yet at the same time I couldn't help feeling guilty about having that feeling. Who was I to wonder who was going to watch a show about—well, what, exactly?—a bunch of rich people who were afraid to fly? After all, here were some of the top minds in television playing with the train set like ten-year-olds, making soft choo-choo sounds and salivating about the possibilities for all the different kinds of cars there would be.

When it finally came on the air in February 1979, *Supertrain* was anything but super. It managed to look cheap despite costing over one million dollars an episode—twice what a normal show was costing at the time. The acting was some of the worst I've ever witnessed outside of *Divorce Court.* The show aired ten times before being pulled off for a retooling. Dan Curtis left after the third episode to regroup and eventually produce more ambitious projects, *Winds of War* and *War and Remembrance,* which he pulled off magnificently. *Supertrain* kept changing under the auspices of new unsuspecting producers before it finally died.

I remember one thing that happened after the new people came in that made me realize there wasn't much hope. I had come up with an idea for a *Supertrain* episode that the producers initially seemed to like. The story involved two young members of the Rockefeller and Vanderbilt families who become engaged, fulfilling the lifelong expectations of their parents. The wedding is to take place in the magnificent grand ballroom on the Supertrain. On the night of the pre-nuptial dinner, however, the groom-to-be is passing through one of the cars when he encounters Cybill Shepherd and immediately falls in love. She then slips away from him, but his life is now completely turned upside down. He must find this beautiful woman somewhere on this huge train. Meanwhile the clock is ticking toward his wedding day. As I said, the new producers seemed to be enthusiastic about developing the idea into a show. They even hired Sam Merrill, the writer I suggested. Then about a month later I ran into Sam and asked him how it was going.

"Oh, fine," he said. "But they did make a few changes in your story."

"Really?" I said. "Like what?"

"Well, instead of the Rockefellers and the Vanderbilts," he said, "the two families are now Basque winegrowers who have been warring with each other for centuries. And instead of the mysterious Cybill Shepherd character, they want him to fall in love with the public relations woman from one of the vineyards. But apart from that . . ."

In the end, that series cost the network a ton of money and further damage to its reputation.

Fred couldn't bear to be reminded of anything about *Supertrain,* including the conference room where we'd all gathered that fateful day. Before he could go in there again, he ordered that the mahogany paneling be stripped off and replaced with light oak. The oval table was replaced, as well as some of the executives who had sat around it oohing and aahing over the train set.

The only success *Supertrain* ever achieved was in France, the country that considers Jerry Lewis a genius.

Traveling the low road on the Supertrain did not result in my worst disaster. For that accomplishment, I took the high road and traveled with some pretty heady company, like Joseph Papp, Elizabeth Swados, Meryl Streep, and Placido Domingo.

On Saturday, January 16, 1981, I scheduled *Alice at the Palace,* a musical adaptation of the *Alice in Wonderland* story starring Ms. Streep, followed by a program called *Live from Studio 8H,* which had Domingo paying homage to the great Enrico Caruso. The three hours of prime-time programming received a *3* in the ratings, making it not just another bad night for NBC but *the lowest-rated night in the history of network television.* Is this conclusive, scientific proof that classical music and other forms of so-called highbrow entertainment are beyond the interest of the mass audience? Absolutely not. It just proves that public television and cable entities such as the A&E Network have a real place on television.

One more word about the business of ideas—emphasis, at last, on business. The creative side of the entertainment industry is vital, but ultimately it must be managed, not spoiled by excess. Ideas may be the precious lifeblood of a network, and they may be difficult to assign a dollar value to, but that doesn't mean there isn't a limit to what each one is worth. There definitely *is* a limit, and a time to say no to the people who try to push you past it. You need to do this for the sake of profit, yes, but also, sometimes, for the sake of pride.

The Cosby Show was probably the single greatest thing that happened at NBC on my watch. I've already described the huge windfall, as well as the psychic satisfactions, it brought to the network, to its star, and to producers Tom Werner and Marcy Carsey. But after *Cosby* was on the air for six years, its contract was up, and we had problems.

The first time I knew there was trouble was when I was chatting with Tom Werner on the set of a then new Carsey-Werner show called *Grand.* Tom and I had known each other

since we were both junior executives at ABC. We had a lot in
common: He and I had graduated from Harvard and Yale
around the same time; we'd hung around together in those
early ABC days, and played in the same friendly touch-foot-
ball games on Sunday mornings. However, just before we
broke off our otherwise-friendly conversation, Tom said,
"We're happy to do a seventh year of *Cosby* for you. But
there's going to be a negotiation. Don't get involved."

Normally, I wouldn't have gotten involved. The network's
head of business affairs, John Agoglia, got to do that fun
stuff, and Tom knew that. It was, all things considered, an
ominous-sounding remark.

A few days after that, I was on an airplane with John when
he brought up *The Cosby Show*. "Brandon, what do you think
they're going to ask for?"

"A lot," I said. "And that irritates me because it's not like
they haven't been amply rewarded as they've gone along.
Another twenty or twenty-five million dollars is what it might
come down to."

John looked slightly nauseated.

The next time I saw him, about a week later, he looked
positively ashen-faced.

"You have no idea what they asked for," he said. "As usual,
the agents and the lawyers put their heads together, and
listen to what they've come up with. They want a hundred-
twenty-five-million-dollar signing bonus. They want to double their licensing fee, and they want substantial other
programming commitments. They're saying the network
made hundreds of millions on Thursday night because of
Cosby and now they want to be compensated."

"Well, that's great," I said. "Tell them that that money has already been boxed up and sent to General Electric, and GE has turned it into light bulbs, airplane parts, and projects for the Defense Department. That money doesn't exist any-more—it's gone. Tell them to get real."

The last thing I wanted to do was lose *The Cosby Show,* and not simply because of what it meant to us financially. I was proud of that half hour of television, and deeply fond of Bill Cosby himself. He was family. Still, I called Bob Wright, who in turn alerted Jack Welch, the chairman of the board of GE, to tell him that as important as *Cosby* was to the network, we might have to reluctantly cut the show loose unless we could achieve a fairer deal. While broadcasting wasn't Jack's pri-mary business, he'd understand what was happening. "This signing bonus alone is ridiculous," I told them. "For that kind of money, we can make one hundred twenty-five pilots. Besides, *Cosby* is starting to slow down in the ratings; next year it will probably only pull a thirty share. If we can't make one thirty-share show with a hundred twenty-five tries," I said, "then believe me, you've got bigger problems than this nego-tiation and the loss of this show."

Bob and Jack agreed with me. "We've got to start planning for a future without this show," Wright said.

The negotiations between our people and theirs dragged on for three months. Then one day I got fed up, and went to New York to see Bill.

It was a Thursday, the day they taped the show, so Norman Brokaw, Bill's longtime agent, and I took a car from the airport and went directly to Bill's dressing room. It was late in the afternoon, the time between the last rehearsal and the taping, and the mood on the set was serene. About the only activity came from Cosby's personal chef, who was cooking us some pasta for an early dinner. Bill sat down on his couch and asked me what was on my mind.

I hadn't prepared a speech, but suddenly heard myself making one. "Bill, I know this deal wasn't your idea," I said, "and I don't want to drag you into it, but ultimately it's your name up there on the show, and whatever happens is going to reflect on you. We're going to try and work it out, but there's a point which we just won't go past. We'll try to get to that maximum point. But if we can't, and your show goes to another network, then we'll do our best to compete against you. In the meantime, I just want to say that you'll never hear a bad word out of my mouth about Bill Cosby, because NBC is blessed to have had six years from you. We benefited from your talents and your vision. You put NBC in the winner's circle, and I'll be in debt to you forever."

Cosby was staring at me intently as I spoke. Then he jumped up, thrust out his chest, and launched into a monologue that was as powerful and wonderful in its own way as the one that had led to his landmark show. *"The Tonight Show* was the first TV show I ever appeared on. Then NBC put me on in *I Spy* in 1965. Nobody had ever had a black lead in a dramatic TV show, but this network took a chance on me. I am going *nowhere."*

A few weeks later such issues as signing bonuses, additional programming commitments, and certain other contractual goodies were no longer part of the negotiations. John Agoglia came into my office and said, "Well, kid, you can breathe easier. We've got the show for next season. Everyone's decided on a fair price to keep the program going forward."

As a connoisseur of good ideas, I appreciated that one.

TEN

···

The BS Factor

I n a sweeping and masterful
work of literature called *Late Night with David Letterman: The
Book,* the famed talk-show host posed the following multiple
choice question:

TV insiders credit NBC's climb to #1 to:

A. actor Bill Cosby
B. executive Brandon Tartikoff
C. a pact with Satan

If you said C, well, you're not alone. I spent a lot of time
during my NBC years trying to convince people that televi-

sion was not entirely the work of the devil. In this regard, one particular incident comes to mind.

The setting: a joint symposium of Harvard and Radcliffe students, midway during my tenure at NBC. On the panel with me are Grant Tinker, Gary David Goldberg, and Alan Horn, the president of Tandem Productions. It had not been an easy afternoon. We all got hammered pretty hard by a bunch of very intelligent young people who called our programming sexist, racist, unimaginative, and just plain dumb. Finally, toward the end of the session, a bearded Harvard student who was sitting in the back row (isn't that where they always are?) stood up and *really* began to attack Grant. "How can you look at yourself in the mirror?" he said. "How can you make peace with the fact that you've taken the most powerful medium of communication known to man and turned it into dreck? Assuming there's a heaven," he went on, "don't you feel that you'll be held accountable at the Pearly Gates for what you've perpetrated?"

Grant was just as angry as the student. "Well, *you* may not like our shows," he said between clenched teeth, "but some of our programming is pretty damn good, and millions and millions of viewers tune in each night to see it. If there is a heaven, I'm sure a lot of those same people will be up there— and I hope to be, too."

Today, this kind of debate is still raging. Do you, as a responsible programmer, fall back on the kind of sugar-coated eye-candy that you think will appeal to a wider audience? Or do you aim to satisfy your more demanding and sophisticated viewers, and perhaps enlighten the rest?

I'm the last person to tell you that ratings aren't vital to a network's health. Network executives have a fiduciary responsibility to deliver the largest possible audience. But every network executive worth his programming tiles knows he has another responsibility as well—a moral and ethical duty to regard the public airwaves with care and thoughtfulness. The airwaves do not belong to you or your networks, they belong to the public.

I had some moments that I was especially proud of at NBC, moments when the Nielsen numbers mattered not. I'm thinking now about *Roe vs. Wade,* a dramatization of the landmark abortion case; *Special Bulletin,* a kind of *War of the Worlds/* CNN-type broadcast about what can happen during a nuclear explosion; *Unnatural Causes,* about the stress syndrome in Vietnam vets; *Love Is Never Silent,* the Emmy Award–winning film that dealt with the isolation of the deaf; and *The Burning Bed,* a film that tackled the then still-taboo subject of spouse abuse.

There were times, though, that I wish I'd been tougher on myself. Times I did have the Nielsen numbers foremost in my mind—and shouldn't have. But when you're deeply involved in a project you can lose perspective. I know now that there are two words that serve as a signal that you're operating in an area of questionable taste. Those words are "Geraldo Rivera."

Before I tell you the story of the Satanism special Geraldo did for NBC in 1988, let me first say that the whole thing was my idea. Sort of. Actually, the part that was my idea was to hire Geraldo. His syndicated specials—digging into Al Capone's vaults, exploring the wreck of the *Titanic*—played on a consortium of affiliates and local stations and they cleaned

our clock. The shows themselves hardly qualified as Great
Moments in Broadcasting; the Capone excavation, as you
may remember, consumed ninety minutes and turned up one
old whiskey bottle. (An inspection of Dana Andrews's old
dressing room could have turned up the same.) But the fact
is, they achieved great ratings, and in many cases it was our
own NBC affiliates who were preempting their regular network programming to broadcast them. It was a case of "If you
can't beat 'em, join 'em." I told Rick Ludwin, NBC's vice-
president of specials and late-night programming, that I'd
rather have Geraldo on my team than continue to compete
against him in a depleted lineup of stations.

In addition, a writers strike hit the industry that summer
and as a result, the premieres of NBC's new fall dramatic
series would be delayed until after the World Series. ABC's
Roseanne, however, was the most touted new series of the
season, and I didn't want to give the show a bye in its opening
two months on the air. Geraldo would be a great blunting
weapon to counter *Roseanne* on its first regular episode after
the pilot.

After the deal was worked out, we had a meeting with
Geraldo, and he presented us with several ideas. The one we
chose, "Satan's Underground," dealt with devil worship and
the sudden increase in satanic cults across the United States.
Yes, from the start it did have a kind of "carny" feel to it, but
this was hardly the first time the subject had been covered on
national TV. One reason we settled on Satanism, in fact, was
that we knew that every time it came up on a news show or a
drama the result was always a high rating. For whatever reason—maybe because they were worried about their kids get-

ting involved, or merely because of the cheap sideshow thrill it provided—a lot of viewers seemed inextricably drawn to this weird topic.

What we didn't count on was that Geraldo was actually going to turn up a lot of shocking stuff. In the back of our minds, I think we assumed he'd give us an hour of somewhat titillating but ultimately unprovocative superficial television. But Geraldo and his investigative team actually went out and found startling evidence of heavy-duty devil worship and satanic acts in the Midwest and Southwest—I'm talking about really disturbing footage. When the Broadcast Standards people saw the show in its original state, they went from initially being speechless to being very vocal indeed. They asked Geraldo to tone it down—a lot—and to diffuse the picture in certain places so the graphic images would be tolerable.

I have to admit, Geraldo was a good soldier about it all. He cooperated with the editing by creating wraparounds (commentary sections that ran before and after each segment of the special) in which he gave Satanism a context, tried to prepare the viewers for what they were about to see. The end result was a show that had been dialed back drastically—but which, in truth, still struck me as too powerful for prime time.

The day before the special was set to air, I called Bob Wright and told him that I was having serious thoughts about the Geraldo show. "I don't know if we should go through with it," I said.

Bob had been equally disturbed by the program cut he'd seen, plus he was back in New York, where he had to quell the uprising of irate sales and financial executives, apoplectic over not being able to sell one commercial to any willing advertiser in this two-hour program.

"Well, check out the situation," Bob said. "And see what our options are."

As it turned out, our options weren't that great. The NBC legal department told me that if we canceled the special at the eleventh hour, Geraldo could say we hadn't lived up to our part of the agreement and had impugned his credentials as a journalist, and he would have a good case if he wanted to sue us. There was another problem, too. Our affiliates, while not being all that excited about getting a questionable Geraldo show nevertheless would not be pleased if we told them we'd changed our minds and were scrapping the broadcast. Remember the old saying "Stuck between a rock and a hard place"? Remember the other one, "The devil made me do it"?

Finally, the day of judgment came. The special was an attempt to get ratings, pure and simple; it was never an attempt to do great TV. Still, I was damned if I did and damned if I didn't, and I knew it. "Let's put this thing on the air," I rationalized. I figured it would all be behind us the next day.

Let me say I've made better decisions in my life.

The next morning I came in and found that *Exposing Satan's Underground* had drawn a huge audience. (To this day, it is the highest-rated nonnews documentary special in network history.) Normally, I would have celebrated a 35 share, but instead I was just glad the whole thing was over. Then, an hour or so later, I found out it wasn't.

Disturbing reports began to trickle in about people inspired by the broadcast to copycat incidents contained in the special. I was appalled. The press focused on those stories and really ripped NBC for putting on such a depraved show. The other side of the coin was the calls and letters our affiliates got thanking NBC for exposing this very real problem that was in their midst, infecting their communities.

If I had to do it all over again, I wouldn't. There aren't thousands of ways to get to 35 share, but there isn't just one, either.

The moral of this story is that it's tough to be your own censor. That's why networks do have a system of checks and balances in which the Broadcast Standards department never reports to programming. This does set up a naturally adversarial relationship, but that's not to say it has to be that way.

I wound up developing something of a close personal relationship with Ralph Daniels, the head of Broadcast Standards for most of my time at NBC. I spoke with him many times during the course of the business week, but because of *Saturday Night Live*'s eleventh-hour deadlines, Ralph left me the number of the restaurant where he'd be eating dinner with his wife, and all the places he'd be over the weekend. I probably made more long-distance calls to Ralph every weekend than I did to my parents in San Francisco.

I've always been amazed at the things that get by—and don't get by—Broadcast Standards. When I worked at ABC, the "BS people," as they're unfortunately known, were extremely strict about eliminating "damn" and "hell." It didn't matter that Rhett Butler had broken certain barriers forty years before; you just couldn't get those words through. The ABC censors also seemed to have absolutely no sense of humor, but the writers didn't mind so much because they could use that to their own advantage. Among the first shows that came under my supervision at ABC was a series called *Dog and Cat,* which was notable only for being the television debut of a young model from Georgia named Kim Basinger. Watching dailies of an episode of the show one afternoon, I saw a take of a scene in which Basinger walks into a police station wearing a slinky, low-cut evening dress through which you could clearly see the outline of her (you should excuse the expression) nipples. Kim's series costar, Lou Antonio, ad-libs a line that fits the situation perfectly. "Hey, is it cold in here?" he says to her, "or are you just glad to see me?" I braced myself for the BS people sitting next to me, but it never came. Because the script hadn't tripped any alarms by using "bad words," and the Mae West allusion was totally lost on the censor types, the line went out over the airwaves.

I got into a lot more hassles later on at NBC, thanks to Steven Bochco. In terms of my workload, Steven giveth, and then he taketh away. He demanded autonomy on *Hill Street* and *L.A. Law,* but because he was always layering his scripts with double entendres, sexual situations, bare skin, and his trademark scatological humor, he, in effect, gave me another job to do—that of liaison with Broadcast Standards. He gave himself a lot of hassles, too. After Bochco and Kozoll submitted the pilot script for *Hill Street* for approval, Broadcast Standards responded with three single-spaced pages of typewritten notes.

Whenever something risqué was slipped into an episode, the BS people would go over each frame in the rough cut like

Jim Garrison scrutinizing the Zapruder film. Sometimes they'd miss rather obvious things—like Furillo telling Davenport that she "gives good succor"—and insist that a scene calling for Furillo and Davenport to take a bath together not be shot unless it was clear they were both wearing clothes in the tub. The occasional absurd scenes *Hill Street* became famous for pale when compared to these kinds of directives. So Bochco began to put in provocative language and scenes that he didn't care about—on purpose. That way, when Broadcast Standards objected to something he thought was important, he could say, "Look, I'll take out these other four things if you give me this, okay?" I don't mean to imply that Bochco invented this ploy, or was the only producer who worked it, but as a tactician he was the best.

Being a pain in the ass was Bochco's hobby and part of his charm. Once, a few years later, *L.A. Law* had a story line in which a representative of a nudist colony goes to a bank to transact some business. Naked, of course. The man walks over to a bank manager's desk, upon which sat a cup of the largest number-two pencils I'd ever seen. The way the shot was set, the pencils became a clever substitute for the proverbial fig leaf. The symbolism, nonetheless, would not be lost on Freud and certainly wasn't lost on the censors.

Bochco claims that he has won 99 percent of his battles with the BS crowd. His longest fight lasted several weeks. It involved a *Hill Street* story line in which Hill and Renko discover a dead man in a hotel room. Shortly thereafter, they hear a bleating sound from the bathroom. When they open the door, they discover a sheep tethered to an overhead pipe.

The sheep has a bow on its head. The fight wasn't about the sheep being there; it was about whether the bow stayed or not. Go figure.

Steven currently has a production deal with ABC, where next year his new series *NYPD Blue* is expected to push television to the R frontier with language and nudity. My suspicion is it'll be PG-13 when the censors get through with it, but it will still be daring, smart television.

No program tested my skill with the censors more than *Saturday Night Live*. There are two reasons *Saturday Night Live* has lasted seventeen years on the air. One is that its impresario, producer Lorne Michaels, ingeniously reinvents and evolves this program, so it never ages.

The second is that the show constantly skirts the danger zone each and every week. Often, I'd be dealing with Broadcast Standards about problems in the upcoming show while taking phone calls from affiliates and sponsors about what had been on the week before. Let's face it, this comes with the territory of doing the only live show of its kind left on television, something Lorne has been resolute about never giving up. Besides, what else can you expect when you're dealing with a cast that is primarily an all-star team of irreverent comics? The funny thing is, for all their griping and moaning, I always got the feeling that the affiliates and the sponsors accepted *Saturday Night Live*. They may not have understood it, but they accepted it. And for a very compelling reason: The show gushed money for them and for NBC. Still, some limits had to be observed.

One night I was sitting at home watching *SNL* when

Charlie Rocket, one of the regular cast members at the time, said the F-word in the middle of a sketch. Now the "Live" in the show's title means just that: There is no tape to cut, no six-second delays or safety net of any kind. So Charlie Rocket's ad-libbed expletive went right over the airwaves into millions of homes. I remained calm; the deed, after all, had been done. But Rocket had to go. TV is like private school. In private school, there are rules about drinking, and if you break those rules, you get expelled. Rocket knew he wasn't supposed to use that language. He used it anyway, and he was out.

Sometimes I'd spend a week arguing about a single word in a script. I remember once when there was an *SNL* sketch containing the word "schmuck," and Broadcast Standards said it had to be cut.

"Why *can't* they say 'schmuck'?" I said to the head censor. "Johnny Carson says 'schmuck' all the time."

"I know what Johnny Carson says," he replied. "But Johnny Carson has a certain stature at NBC. He's been here more than twenty-five years. He can say 'schmuck.' When these people have been here that long, they can say 'schmuck,' too."

The *SNL* sketch that gave me the most grief, however, was the Jew/Not-a-Jew game show. Tom Hanks played the host. A slide of a famous personality would appear on the screen, and the panelists had to decide whether the person was Jewish. "Our first famous personality," Hanks said, affecting in his best game-show-host voice, "is Penny Marshall, the affable star of television's *Laverne & Shirley*! Okay, panelists, Jew or Not a Jew?" After the panelists locked in their answers, the sketch cut to a fake commercial, a parody of those "IBM invites you to make the call" spots: "Sandy Koufax is on the mound for the Los Angeles Dodgers, Game Seven of the World Series against the Minnesota Twins. The stylish left-hander is involved in a tense battle with the score locked at two to two. Okay, IBM invites you to make the call. Sandy Koufax—Jew, Not a Jew?" Then they cut back to Hanks, who announced that Penny Marshall was really Italian, and gave the winners their rewards.

It was funny, I thought—but was it anti-Semitic? All week long, I agonized over that question, not just with Broadcast Standards but with myself. Since I'm Jewish, I wondered if I was being too sensitive or maybe too blasé. If this was about Italians, would I think it was awful? *Should* I think it was awful? Finally, a few hours before airtime, I took a deep breath and conferred with the Standards people, and we decided to go with it.

The morning after controversial material is aired on television is usually taken up with a flood of phone calls—most of them negative (when was the last time you made a phone call when you *liked* something?). In this case, it was Sunday morning, I was home, and still my phone rang off the hook. Of the many calls I received, the one I remember best was from my mother. "I cannot believe it," she said. "I'm embarrassed to call you my son. This was the most anti-Semitic thing I've ever seen." Then she paused. "Besides, I always thought Penny Marshall *was* Jewish!"

ELEVEN

....

Hello, I Must
Be Going

I
t all seemed just a little
unusual that morning in May of 1990 at the Waldorf-Astoria
in New York City.

Not the being there. I had been there ten times before to
announce NBC's new fall prime-time schedule. Did I feel
different this time because I hadn't stayed up all night writing
and rewriting my five opening ad-libs, frantically calling my
friend Jim Stein, an Emmy Award–winning comedy writer, to
punch up my material at three o'clock in the morning? Was
I just a little too unwired? Or was it because this time I
wouldn't be the sole master of ceremonies as I had been in
the past? This time I would be sharing the podium with

Warren Littlefield (soon to be announced president of NBC
Entertainment) and Perry Simon, our senior vice president of
prime-time programs.

Or was it because I wasn't giddy with excitement to be
welcoming the dozen or so stars from our new fall series?
They were waiting backstage to be unveiled to the twelve
hundred members of the media and advertising communities
sitting in the audience. One of them, young Will Smith, the
star of *Fresh Prince of Bel Air,* was particularly keyed. He was,
after all, about to be born, in a sense, into a whole new phase
of his show business career.

Will Smith wasn't a discovery of mine. The music world and
the NBC programming team was way ahead of me there. But
at that moment I felt a personal connection to Will, a mixture
of the paternal and the nostalgic that caused me to walk over
and put a hand on his shoulder.

"I hope you know who your friends are, Will," I told him.
"Because in this coming year you're going to have a lot more
people wanting to be your friend than you could ever imagine."

Without missing a beat, Will recounted a similar (well, sort
of) conversation he recently had with Eddie Murphy.

"You know, Eddie told me if I'm a hit, I should get ready
for three rumors that always follow black guys when they get
famous: You're on drugs. You're gay. Or you spent all your
money and now you're broke."

Street smarts are street smarts. There's no disputing that.

Suddenly NBC's theme music was being piped into the
ballroom: "NBC. The place to be." Almost twenty years
before, I was at a similar event, only it was at ABC in Los

Angeles. The theme then? "ABC. The place to be." Wasn't this where I came in?

The year before, someone on my staff had spoken up at a meeting and said, "There's a whole thing going on out there with home video cameras, and we ought to do something about it. We ought to try to somehow make this trend into a show."

"We did it already," I said. "And it didn't work."

Five years earlier, when my daughter was a toddler, Lilly and I had bought a video camera—one of those early, unwieldy models—and we became enthralled. From our own experience, I got the idea for a one-hour special showcasing home videos with Michael J. Fox as host. We hoped a large segment of Americans would be fascinated by each other's home movies the way Lilly and I were with ours of Calla. They weren't. The show pulled a 14 share. But one year after my plugged-in staff member made his suggestion, ABC aired *America's Funniest Home Videos.* (*They* used a sitcom star, too. In this case, Bob Saget.) The show became a megahit. Times had changed. Video cameras and VCRs had reached a critical mass and the elusive audience had drifted, yet again, and finally embraced the concept. But why hadn't I been watching?

Before, I had been ahead of my time. Now I was behind the times, caught in a vise on Sunday night at 8:00, between *Murder She Wrote* (for the mature audience) on CBS and *America's Funniest Home Videos* (for the younger audience) on ABC.

Several months before the Waldorf extravaganza, Bob Wright and I had attended the annual meetings of the National Association of Television Programming Executives in Houston. But in addition to the agenda on the program, I had one of my own.

"This is my last time around the league," I told Bob at a meeting in his hotel room. "I think it's time for me to leave. I've done the job for twelve years, and every year in this job is like dog years—each year feels like seven. My original inner circle has moved on, and I'm starting to feel like Peter Pan. Every fall I greet a new batch of eager young faces at the staff meeting, all expecting me to take them to Never-Never Land. Well, maybe it's time for me to grow up."

Bob's a savvy guy. He had doubtless sensed my restlessness before this conversation and couldn't have been more gracious. Inevitably, our talk drifted to my future plans. I had been seriously considering a venture into independent production—which was an iffy proposition, as both he and I knew. The entire entertainment industry was then on hold, waiting for the FCC to render a decision on the Fin-Syn rules, which set limits on the percentage of programming that a network could own. Still, I assumed that whatever the ruling, independent production would still be a lucrative pursuit for me. I wanted to follow through on some of my own ideas as a producer, instead of trying to persuade others to execute them. And I had several series commitments accrued at NBC to give me some advantage and security in what I knew was a risky venture nonetheless.

Bob asked me my timetable, and I told him June—six months. But he asked me for an extra year to effect a more orderly transition. How could I say no to a person who had let me operate with total creative autonomy for five years?

From his first day on the job, Bob Wright had sensed that an in-house production studio was the last growth opportunity left to the networks. So my final challenge at NBC would be to fortify NBC Productions. Working in tandem with John Agoglia, I would try to point them toward the future before I set sail on my own course. There seemed to be an appropriate symmetry to this.

One night during my last summer at NBC, Lilly and I went out to eat in a little Beverly Hills restaurant called La Dolce Vita. When we walked in I spotted Gary Goldberg holding court at a table with several notables, among them Joseph Heller, the author of *Catch-22*. Heller's novel was the bible of the absurdist generation I belong to. Since my other two favorite authors at college, Thomas Pynchon and J. D. Salinger, had virtually gone into hiding, here was my only shot at meeting one of my true literary heroes.

After Gary introduced us, Heller began pumping me about my job. He seemed fascinated by all it entailed. How long had I been doing it? How old was I now? When I told him, a smile crept onto his face. He turned to Lilly and whispered, "I feel sorry for you. Your husband is going to have the biggest midlife crisis anyone has ever seen."

Later that summer I visited someone who never had a midlife crisis. He never had the time; he was always on the road, entertaining people, making them laugh, raising money for worthwhile causes, giving of himself. Bob Hope was an NBC legend. He had been with the network for over fifty years. Having an annual one-on-one lunch with Bob was intimidating in the early years of my tenure, but over time, I developed a kind of kinship with him. In the fickle, high-turnover show business swirl, even I, with twelve years at the network, qualified as an NBC survivor.

Weeks in advance of our lunches at his Toluca Lake digs, I would stockpile all the great jokes I'd recently heard so I could try to one-up him (an impossible task, I knew from experience, but still, I tried). During this particular lunch it was business as usual. I tried to match him and he flattened me. But somehow, he must have sensed I was in transition.

I'd been to Bob's house at least a dozen times before that afternoon, but this time he decided to let me into his inner sanctum. After dessert, he led me to a vault and dialed the combination. Inside were rows upon rows of alphabetized file cabinets.

"What's in there, Bob?" I asked.

"Riches, Brandon. That's where I keep my jokes."

Bob proceeded to open up the "H" drawer and took out a manila folder marked "Horseracing." Inside were stacks of typewritten pages of jokes about jockeys, lame mares, etc.

"You know Bob, you could clear out this whole room. Put all this stuff on a computer disc."

"Now why would I do something like that? Everything I need, I know where to find—right now."

So much for bringing the computer age to a luminary who is ageless.

Next Bob took me into his office. He opened up a large envelope and handed me some photos.

"I was going through my drawers and I found these. They're something else, aren't they?"

The photos were ones he had taken when he and the Allied

troops were allowed into a concentration camp days after the war ended. He told me about the horrors he had seen, the Holocaust memories that have haunted him since that day.

On the walk back to my car, Bob and I resumed quibbling about his fall special and its guest bookings (I lobbied for the Fresh Prince and Seinfeld, he for Brooke Shields and funny man Jack Carter). Then I thanked him for lunch, gave him the kind of hug you'd give your grandfather, and wistfully drove away. Little did I know that a year later, Bob's and my history would intersect again, this time at the film studio where he began his career.

When Stanley Jaffe, the newly appointed chief operating officer of Paramount Communications, called in the spring of 1991, he was not the first person to talk to me about heading up a movie studio. Fay Vincent, now the commissioner of baseball, approached me in 1986 when he was the top executive at Columbia Pictures. And Kirk Kerkorian pursued me to run his MGM-UA operation in 1988. I resisted both opportunities because my gut instinct told me the ongoing turmoil at both of these studios was not going to be quelled by my either being hired or by my being successful there. (Both studios changed ownership before the decade ended).

Whatever I didn't know about the movie business—which was a lot—Stanley Jaffe could teach me, and teach me well. In undertaking the challenge of turning around a movie studio, it's essential to have a more than equal partner in the boat with you. In addition, thanks to Martin Davis, Paramount Communications chairman and CEO, the studio was one of the few that remained in American hands. And it was

also one of the few studios, regardless of nationality of ownership, that had the deep pockets to ride out the inevitable
swings at the box office.

So I had finally come to a crossroads, about to leave NBC,
a place I'd both grown up in and helped grow. Somehow, I'd
experienced this moment before, but the last time, it was
someone else who was wrestling with the career choices he
had made.

Ten years before, almost to the day, Dick Ebersol had taken
over as producer of *Saturday Night Live* after Jean Doumanian
departed. I had come to the set to wish Dick and guest host
Chevy Chase well, and to watch the show from the producer's
booth overlooking the set. I was the only one there, until the
door swung open and in walked John Belushi. Belushi had
left the cast some time before. He was alone, and somehow,
without his *Saturday Night* colleagues around, he seemed a
little lost. It wasn't long, though, before he found an obviously expensive bottle of French wine, a good-luck gift for
Dick from some well-meaning sycophant. Belushi yanked the
gift card from the bottle, pushed the cork in with his finger,
took a drink, and handed the bottle to me.

As the show progressed, we passed the bottle back and
forth and got to talking. We discovered we were both suburban kids of about the same age. Both of us had been class
clowns, inveterate wise-asses who'd pulled our own share of
memorable pranks and gotten into trouble with authority
figures.

It struck me then how we'd taken such different paths.
Here I was, a network executive wearing my go-to-work suit

and tie on a Saturday night, and there he sat, a self-destructive comic genius, unshaven, in his blue jeans and T-shirt.

"I should never have left the show. It was the best fucking time of my life," Belushi said, not knowing how prophetic this would be. "*I* should be up there right now. Not Chevy."

Somewhere along the line we had both made our choices.

By the end of April 1991, I had made yet another. I was going to Paramount.

TWELVE

....

TV 2000

When I was twenty-two and working at WTNH in New Haven, we once had the Amazing Kreskin on one of our talk shows. Kreskin astounded the live studio audience with his inexplicable feats of mentalism, telling them secrets about themselves and correctly indicating where they'd hidden certain objects on the set. I was truly impressed, and I went up to him right after the show to tell him so.

I introduced myself as the station's promotion manager and said, "Wow, you were great."

"Thanks, kid," he said. "Hey—can you tell me where the men's room is?"

For a long moment I just stood there, stunned.

"You mean," I finally said, "you don't *know?*"

The moral of that poignant and touching little tale is that life is a series of rude awakenings. Success is a matter of how smoothly and how wisely you adjust to the shock of the new.

It's been a little over a year now since I left the catbird seat at a television network. And though I'm still personally involved in the birthing of shows such as the new *Untouchables* and *The Middle Ages,* my job at Paramount has given me a new perspective. I knew the TV business was changing. But I never realized just how fundamental those changes would be, or how fast the future was rushing toward us.

In many ways, the future is already here.

Let me tell you just one more story.

In 1986, NBC changed hands, and I came up for my first business review under the new GE management. The meeting was held at the Beverly Hilton in Los Angeles. As I sat down at the big oval table in one of the hotel's conference rooms, across from Jack Welch, the chairman of GE, and Bob Wright, the newly appointed president of NBC, I was fairly confident. After six years on the job, I felt the network was cooking about as well as it ever had been. We were number one in prime time for the first time in thirty years; we were number one on Saturday morning for the fourth year in a row; we were number one in late night, as we had been since the advent of Johnny Carson; and in daytime, while we weren't the leader, our ratings were the most competitive they'd been in ten years, and the demographics were improving. I was, to put it mildly, psyched—and rather proud of the slide show of

. . . .

charts, graphs, and sales projects that were about to flash before the eyes of my new bosses.

The lights went down. The dog and pony show began. And in ten minutes I found out how "Neutron Jack" Welch got his name.

Jack waited for the entertainment division presentation to finish. Then he asked for the slide carousel to be reset so we could review certain financial graphs.

The first one he asked for illustrated the cost of all our programming—everything from *The Tonight Show* to *Hill Street Blues*. Because we had such popular shows, the actors, producers, and studios involved in making them knew that money was coming in through the windows at NBC, and many of those people were renegotiating their contracts. This meant that our costs were going up.

Next, Jack said he wanted to take another look at the sales figures. Even he had to admit those weren't bad—at the moment. His long-range projections, however, showed sales leveling off, and even tapering down during the rest of the decade.

Then the lights came up.

"I know you're feeling pretty good about what you've done," Jack said. "But you have to go beyond the ratings, go past the moment. Do that, and you'll see that your costs are going up at a far greater rate than your sales increases. Eventually what's going to happen is that your cost line is going to meet and then cross your sales line. And then what?"

Jack paused a beat and said, "Brandon, every morning you ought to get down on your knees and thank the good Lord that the Japanese haven't figured out a way to make a cost-effective American television show. Because when they do, you're going to be out of business."

I was stunned and initially a little angry. After all, I'd been expecting a hearty pat on the back. I might still be kind of ticked off—if the conditions that Jack described that day hadn't basically come to pass.

In the late 1980s, the Big Three networks hit a financial wall. Not only was the recession depressing their ad sales, but competition from cable, VCRs, the Fox network, and the proliferation of independent stations was eroding the audience that CBS, NBC, and ABC had once divvied up almost exclusively among themselves.

Talk about rude awakenings: By 1990, *L.A. Law* could—and did—become a top-ranked show with more or less the same Nielsen numbers that another quality legal drama, *The Defenders,* was canceled for in 1965. Hit shows like *Star Trek: The Next Generation* and *Oprah* didn't even *need* a traditional network to succeed; they reached their audience via syndication. With so much competition, networks, for the first time in history, no longer found it easy to turn a profit; whereas once even the third-place finisher did well for itself financially, now the *winner* of the ratings race was losing money.

Something has to change, right?

Not exactly.

Something has already changed, and it's time to face the facts.

The mass audience is an endangered species, and one not likely to make a comeback. The future is in Queens, New York, where cable subscribers are living in a 150-channel universe. What you'll find there—and what you'll soon find almost everywhere—are many splinter groups of viewers watching shows that appeal to their specialized interests and tastes.

How will the medium survive with such scaled-down numbers? With proper management, quite well. Because for the first time, networks and independent stations will be able to deliver to their advertisers the kind of viewers—and *only* the kind of viewers—that fit the customer profile for, say, BMWs or Obsession perfume or Guess jeans.

This trend toward niche-marketing is already happening in the magazine and retail clothing businesses. Truth be told, it's already happening on TV, where one can watch, for example, The Movie Channel, the Weather Channel, ESPN, and Fox, an over-the-air network aimed almost exclusively at the eighteen-to-thirty-four-year-old crowd. Someday soon we'll likely see an entire network aimed at older viewers, showing health and financial news intermingled with nostalgic variety shows and reruns of *Matlock* and *Murder, She Wrote*.

While this trend constitutes real progress, it also has a downside. We may soon lose forever the sense of shared experience we as a nation had back when, say, the Beatles were making their first appearance on *Ed Sullivan* or when, more recently, we all seemed to be talking about Murphy Brown's baby. Yes, such breaking news as elections, the Gulf War, and the Clarence Thomas hearings, and such sports events as the World Series and Super Bowl, may still bring a sizable audience together to watch history happen. But with more and more sets in every home, and more channels to choose from, TV-watching will become an increasingly isolated experience.

The good news is that the quality of television will get better—and I'm not just talking about the high-definition sets that will have us watching crystal-clear, movie-screen-quality images within the next decade. No, what I mean is that there will be a substantial improvement in TV-show *content.*

Consider: In the original Golden Age of TV, and for years thereafter, the industry was governed to a great degree by the theory of L.O.P., or Least Objectionable Programming. What this said in essence was that people picked a show in any given time period not because they liked it, but because they didn't hate it as much as the other shows that were on the air. At a time when TV was still something of a novelty and there weren't many channels to choose from, you, as a programmer, could rely on L.O.P. to get you through the night. Today, though, the idea is about as current as a rabbit-ears antenna. If a viewer is sitting there with a remote control in one hand, and a TV-listings guide showing several dozen selections in the other, they'd *better* have some reason to stay tuned to your show. In the future, instead of L.O.P., we'll have . . . well, let's call it S.F.T.S., for Somebody's Favorite Television Show. And to be that—to be the kind of program that a viewer is going to look forward to, and build his or her evening around—programmers are going to need to give the audience something special.

But viewers won't be shaping their schedules around network programming forever. For a decade now we've had VCRs, which allow viewers to capture and replay at their convenience shows that have already been broadcast. In the not-very-distant future, we're going to go several steps further. Someday, maybe even *before* the year 2000, you'll come home from a hard day at the office, flip on your computer, and fire up a video menu. Let's say you're in the mood to watch *Northern Exposure*. Working with your remote-control device, you'll be able to preview scenes from the series, or call up brief plot descriptions, from five available episodes. Later that night you can watch the news—not just the news that some local station wants to feed you, but a selection of reports listed on the video menu and pretailored, based on past viewing habits, to your interests. After that, you can round out the night with a movie—one of several thousand available titles.

What the future of television comes down to, ultimately, is a great power shift—away from the networks and toward the viewers. Instead of someone like me deciding what goes on the air—and when—you'll be making the decision for yourself. You, too, can be your own television programmer, your own Ed Sullivan. You'll be able to turn on whatever acts and wonders turn *you* on.

I hope you have as much fun as I did.

Go for it.

ACKNOWLEDGMENTS

I'd like to thank some people who got me here—living and writing what became this book.

In local television there were Mal Potter, Pete Orne, and Bob King in my New Haven days, and Lew Erlicht, Chris Duffy, John Severino, and Dick O'Leary in Chicago.

My first year in network television at ABC was exhilarating because it was the network's first full season in first place, and because people like Brandon Stoddard, Cliff Alsberg, and the late Steve Gentry weren't so busy succeeding they couldn't tell me where I was failing.

I spent fourteen years at NBC, so my "thank you" list is understandably longer.

A C K N O W L E D G M E N T S

....

In New York, I'd like to thank Ray Timothy, Pier Mapes, Bob Walsh, Irwin Segelstein, Bob Blackmore, Don Carswell, Ed Scanlon, Bob Niles, Bob Butler, Gerry Jaffe, Katie Fitch, Dorothy Worthington, and my scheduler of schedulers, Lee Currlin, who all made my time at 30 Rock so rich. And I can personally vouch that Tom Brokaw, Bryant Gumbel, Bob Costas, and Jane Pauley are people you want in your lifeboat.

On the West Coast, I'll confine my thanks to those who aren't already mentioned in these pages: John McMahon, Perry Lafferty, Susan Baerwald, Fenton Coe, Gene Walsh, Joe Cicero, Paul King, Steve White, Garth Ancier, Leslie Lurie, Deanne Barkley, Lori Openden, Sue Binford, the late Jay Michelis, Kathy Tucci, and Paul Wang. I was also blessed with the three best promotion minds in the business today: Steve Sohmer, John Miller, and Vince Manze.

The Affiliate Board members I came to know knew a lot and passed that knowledge on to me (whether I wanted to hear it or not). Special thanks to Eric Bremner, Fred Paxton, Jim Lynagh, Jim Sefert, Bob "Suitcase" Sutton, Bruce McGorrill, and Jon Ruby.

In the Fat Chance Department, television critics Bill Carter, Tom Shales, Eric Mink, and Rick DuBrow tried to keep me honest. And Ken Auletta tried to keep me famous.

"Dinosaurs" David Gerber, Edgar Scherick, and Lee Rich made me appreciate good stories and picking up the check.

Financial and spiritual advisors Michael Ovitz, Ken Ziffren, Jeff Katzenberg, and Larry Angen made me appreciate the difference between good deals and bad ones (they only represented the former).

A c k n o w l e d g m e n t s

Thanks to my unique doctor/friend Dennis Slamon, for keeping me and Calla alive.

Thanks to my sister, Lisa, who tolerated a sibling who needed all the attention.

Thanks to True Blues like Larry Lyttle, Jim Stein, Jimmy Burrows, Dick Ebersol, Ronnie Rubenstein, Fred Richman, Michael Zinberg, Skip Freedman, Richard Tuggle, Jon Friedland, and Don Ohlmeyer who told me they'd still love me even if they weren't featured prominently in these pages.

Thanks to Helen Kushnick for telling me to do a book, and thanks to Joni Evans for agreeing.

Thanks to Turtle Bay staffers Karen Rinaldi and Jason Kaufman and my helpers Barbara Barry, Rick Riggs, and Sarah Barrett for physically "getting it done."

Thanks to my original partner, Steve Oney, who left me for Leo Frank, but introduced me to his (and now my) agent, Kathy Robbins. Steve, you're still the best clutch hitter I know.

Thanks to my editor, Susan Kamil, and my collaborator, Charlie Leerhsen: You were both patient when I left you no choice and impatient when I needed prodding. But you were always inspired and always there for me.

My father taught me the value of hard work and, thanks to Fred Silverman, Grant Tinker, Bob Wright, the late Thornton Bradshaw, and Jack Welch, I experienced its rewards.

INDEX

....

BRANDON TARTIKOFF is chairman of Paramount Pictures. He lives with his wife, Lilly, and their daughter, Calla, in Beverly Hills, California.

CHARLES LEERHSEN, a senior writer at *Newsweek* for eleven years, is now a senior editor at *People*. He coauthored *Trump: Surviving at the Top* with Donald Trump and *Press On: Further Adventures in the Good Life* with Chuck Yeager. He has also written articles for *Esquire, Rolling Stone, TV Guide,* and *Premiere.*